All Children are Special

All Children are Special

CREATING AN INCLUSIVE CLASSROOM

Greg Lang and Chris Berberich

Foreword by Gretchen Goodman

Stenhouse Publishers

YORK, MAINE

Stenhouse Publishers, 226 York Street, York, Main 03909

1995 by Christine Berberich and Greg Lang

ISBN 1-57110-017-2

Published simultaneously in the United States
by Stenhouse and in Australia by
Eleanor Curtain Publishing
906 Malvern Road
Armadale, Australia 3143

Production by Sylvana Scannapiego, Island Graphics
Edited by Ruth Siems
Cover design by David Constable
Text design and page make-up by Patricia Tsiatsias
Printed in Australia by Impact Printing Pty Ltd

Contents

Acknowledgements   viii

Foreword by Gretchen Goodman   ix

Introduction   1

Chapter 1: Stories from the classroom   3
    Everyone is different   3
    Stories from the playground   7
    Social skills   11

Chapter 2: What is inclusion?   16
    Setting a context   16
    The inclusive classroom   18

Chapter 3: Creating an inclusive learning environment   23
    Building blocks of inclusion   23
    Inclusive climates: the classroom environment   28

Chapter 4: Managing the environment   36
    Learning principles   36
    Management and organisation   41

Chapter 5: Strategies for teaching and learning   52
    Collaborative learning   52
    Curriculum adaptation   64
    Individual education programs   69

Chapter 6: Raising awareness: preparing for inclusion   85
    Awareness meetings   86
    The importance of recording   91
    Sharing information   98

Chapter 7: Supporting inclusive practice   104
    Personal support systems   105
    Inclusive practice   110
    Parents are special too   112
    The physical world   116

Glossary   122

Blackline masters   123

References and resources   136

Index   139

If...

If a child can't talk, we can explore an amazing range of voice output devices ...

If a child can't walk, we can measure them up for some wheels ...

If a child can't remember, we can devise cues and picture systems to help ...

If a child can't hear, we can learn to sign ...

If a child can't socialise appropriately, we can model kindness, self-discipline and love ...

If a child can't sit still and learn, we can plan for movement and activity-based lessons ...

If a child can't go to the toilet unaided, we can take the time to help ...

If a child can grasp your hand, or smile, or sign 'Thankyou', then what else is there to ask for?

There are no endings, just new doors to open ...

Acknowledgements

We would like to acknowledge that the idea for *All Children Are Special* and the final putting together was aided by many people.

We particularly acknowledge and thank those special children whose lives have touched our own — their sense of wonder and community, and their courage, inspire many whose everyday lives are so much easier.

The children at Holy Cross School, Wooloowin, have shared learnings, lives, hopes and dreams, and were the catalysts for *All Children Are Special*. Their parents have supported our efforts with generosity and we thank them for their time and care.

A very special thank you to colleagues, and teachers and students in many schools who have provided ideas, feedback and inspiration.

There are people to acknowledge for their patience and understanding as we struggled to find the time to write amidst family, work and study commitments — Therese, Julian, Madeleine, Maria, Jochen, Mark, Christopher and Jonathon.

And to Sara and Erin, two special friends — thank you for your smiling faces on our cover.

Foreword

Public school educators in the United States are being challenged with a paradigm shift in how they deliver special education. Prior to 1975, any child who walked through our classroom doors with a special need or label quickly found his or her way to a special education classroom to join us during art, music, physical education, lunch, or recess, but only if they had proved to us that they could 'fit in' during those times. Special education was a location rather than a service.

The Education for All Handicapped Children Act of 1975 (PL 94–142) and its successor, the Individuals with Disabilities Act (IDEA), passed in 1990, instituted a much needed change. Both mandates stipulate that any child with disabilities must be provided a free and appropriate public education in the least restrictive environment possible. This means that children with disabilities must be educated to the maximum extent possible with their nondisabled age-appropriate peers. IDEA also requires schools to establish procedures that guarantee that every child with special needs will receive an education within a regular classroom environment, using supplementary aides or services as necessary, unless the nature or degree of the student's need makes satisfactory education in this manner impossible.

Inclusion today has become a universal human rights movement to end the former debilitating practice of excluding children from the regular education environment based on physical needs, learning styles, and psychological and physiological differences. With all children being accepted as equal members of the learning circle, not just for some special classes or portions of the day but to the maximum extent possible, a regular classroom teacher may understandably feel a bit of panic: How can I care for these children properly? I don't know enough. I haven't been trained.

All Children Are Special helps classroom teachers face this challenge. Although the authors of this book are Australian, their philosophy and sentiments parallel those of American educators. Greg Lang and Chris Berberich demonstrate that the core of inclusion — an acceptance and appreciation of both the diversity and the uniqueness of the individual learner — is universal and that methods used to achieve inclusion in Australia are equally effective in the United States, and vice versa. Educators in both countries hold to the importance of all children learning together, differently abled students side by side with their age-appropriate peers, for all or a majority of the educational and social day. Educators in both countries acknowledge the importance of collaboration and cooperation between and among teachers, parents, and the community in order to enhance student success while developing learning opportunities as individual as each learner's strengths and needs. In both countries, supplemental supports and aides are used within the regular education classroom and the power of building-based teams is viewed as a cornerstone of the inclusion principle.

Differences in the approaches toward inclusive practices in the United States and Australia have more to do with innate educational structures and with cultural practices than with the human rights of those *within* the educational structure.

For example, Lang and Berberich may refer to a grade assignment as 'year five.' In terms of typical grade assignments in the United States, this corresponds to a fifth year in school, or, typically, a fourth-grade assignment. (For those fortunate educators who have moved beyond lock-step grade assignments, this corresponds to the continuous progress of a nine-year-old.) Also, in Australia, school years are divided into 'terms' rather than semesters or quarters; special educators are described as support personnel or support officers; and occupational therapy or physical therapy is generally provided as a pull-out service (it's typically a push-in service in the United States). American educators will also notice slight procedural differences in how Australian children move from one educational setting to another.

Culturally, there are differences in medical responsibilities and in toileting procedures. In the United States, medicine is normally administered only by school nurses or similar medically approved personnel, and toileting and other self-help skills are typically not the responsibility of the classroom teacher. There are also differences in data gathering, team planning and the roles of team members, and evaluating procedures. (Though as to that, we need only remind ourselves that in the United States many inclusion procedures vary greatly not only from state to state, but from one school district to another.)

The theory and methods offered here easily transcend these minor educational and cultural differences. Lang and Berberich reveal their heartfelt sentiments and daily struggles in their journey from being individual teachers assigned to specific learning populations to becoming successful collaborators developing inclusive classrooms and quality education for all learners. This book is an outstanding resource of philosophy, practical approaches, teacher-tested adaptations and blackline masters. It is a resource applicable to teachers just beginning to work in an inclusion classroom, to teachers hitting their first roadblock on the journey and to teachers seeking to make the experience ever more successful.

The honesty and emotion of these Australian educators, vividly supplemented by the personal anecdotes of teachers and students in inclusion classrooms, help all of us realize not only that *All Children Are Special* but that all education is special.

Gretchen Goodman

Introduction

This book is the result of a desire to provide a resource for an increasingly large number of teachers and schools faced with the complexities of teaching and providing for children with special needs. By *special needs*, we refer primarily to those children whose physical and/or intellectual capacities have been affected to some degree, so that their participation in teaching and learning situations requires assistance or modification.

We asked ourselves: Is it possible to see spina bifida as a situation, rather than as a condition or affliction? See it as a situation that perhaps requires different learning strategies, physical adaptations or *attitudes* on the part of educators?

Inclusion is both the goal and the method by which teachers create a classroom that values the special needs child and helps them to feel secure, and appreciated for who they are and what they can contribute. Part of the philosophy behind an inclusive classroom is a belief that all people have something to learn and gain from understanding and appreciating others. Some might call it human interconnectedness — a sense that we all need one another, and this interdependence is critical to our survival.

Over the past decade there has been increasing awareness of the interrelationship of human beings to the wider global community and its networks of living and non-living things. There is a saying that we cannot understand another person until we walk in their shoes. Inclusive classrooms deliberately promote knowledge and understanding of what it is like, to be in the 'other person's shoes'.

The inclusive classroom is one that is safe, open and yet challenging — because inclusion is not necessarily the usual way of society. We have witnessed a growth in rights and responsibilities of all types of people who are in some way disadvantaged. Parents of special needs children are more vocal about access and provision for their children in 'regular' schools. We have come beyond mainstreaming (placing disabled children in regular classrooms) to a point where the real needs and issues related to the whole classroom are considered in the provision of an education for special needs children.

This book is both theoretical and informative, but at its heart is a belief and a knowledge that we *can* make a difference in the educational process. We believe that there are four distinct elements to building the inclusive classroom.

1 Creating a learning environment that is safe, accepting and caring, where differences are seen as challenges and opportunities for growth.

2 Utilising strategies for teaching and learning that maximise each child's participation, development and interaction.

3 Managing the classroom and school environment to best provide for special needs children.

4 Becoming aware of the wider issues, such as parent involvement, networks, support people, and attitudinal development.

All Children Are Special will help anyone concerned for or involved in the teaching of special needs children to understand the philosophy behind, and the practicalities involved in, providing inclusive education. It is our hope that readers will be better equipped to create an inclusive classroom and a quality education for all involved.

Stories from the classroom

Everyone is different

Carmel has Down's syndrome. The way she looks, walks and talks tells us that we should expect to modify her classwork so she will be able to participate happily and handle the tasks.

Kelly's wheelchair is an indicator of her physical limitations and is a cue that learning may be difficult.

Anna's frown tells us that she is having trouble understanding what she is being asked to do. Her teachers need to allow what they call 'Anna time', because it takes her considerable time to change from one learning situation to another. Changes happening too quickly usually result in explosive verbal interactions, followed by a sulky withdrawal from the group.

All these children have instantly recognisable special needs. We suggest that these more extreme learning needs are more likely to be catered for in inclusive, cooperative classrooms, where the learning environment is more flexible and open than could be the case in traditional classrooms. We also suggest that **all children have 'special' learning or social needs** of one kind or another.

What about me?

Our children will struggle daily in classrooms if we as teachers are not sufficiently aware, or skilled in understanding the complexities of social and learning interactions. Given the wide range of home and community backgrounds from which our school clientele comes, perhaps we need to reconsider our teaching practice in the light of *meeting the needs*. Teachers need to be able to employ a varied and engaging repertoire of teaching and learning strategies.

The following stories tell of many different types of learners, each with their own very special needs.

The teacher who insists on doing things one way only, all the time, year after year, cannot meet the needs of today's learners. As society changes what needs to be learned, and moulds young learners by media and technology, so too must teachers adapt and change. After all, we are in the future's market. Problem-solving, divergent thinking, and risk-taking should be part of our classroom business, every single day.

Not paying attention again ...

Justin is one of a great number of children in our schools who have a slight hearing loss. He often seems to be inattentive and frustrates his class teacher by 'ignoring' instructions. He usually needs to be asked more than once before he responds to questions. Justin is a bright little boy who looked forward to going to school. His imagination transports him to places where interesting people are good company, and exciting events occur.

His parents are very aware of the difficulties Justin may experience because of his hearing impairment. They have spoken with the class teacher, suggesting the most suitable position in class for Justin to sit, where he would be most likely to hear as well as he is able. It has been frustrating for Justin's parents to learn that no changes have been made to the seating arrangements, even though a whole term has gone by.

Simple solutions, like changing the place where a child sits, are perhaps too simple. Are we teachers too sceptical to believe in such an obvious change making a difference? Do we choose to believe that children presenting with learning difficulties, either physical or intellectual, are too hard for us to handle?

'I wonder what it takes to make you pay attention, Justin!' says the teacher. Justin is looking out the window. It is almost time for lunch.

'I wonder if Peter has told Wendy and the lost boys about his new plans for playtime ...' he thinks to himself.

Daniel's always last

Daniel is in year 6 this year. He spends a great deal of time at school feeling unhappy. Playtime is best because the boys mostly play soccer, and he knows he is good at running and kicking.

Schooltime is not so good! Daniel is usually last to complete written tasks, especially when he has to copy from the blackboard. There is no particular label for Dan's difficulties. When Dan started school, the teacher was aware that he was experiencing problems and seemed to take longer than other children to complete a task. School funding did not allow for a therapy program at school, so Dan's parents sought help through the public health system. He has since received blocks of occupational and speech therapy sessions.

Outside school time, Dan's parents also take him to gymnastics, and he is a keen member of the local soccer club. Recently, he was enrolled in a term's drama classes, which he absolutely hated! Speaking out in front of others, and remembering what to say at the right time was very difficult for him.

The drama teacher suggested that he invite a friend along for a lesson or two. John was the obliging friend and was happy to help out. He had a wonderful time, but Dan still became very distressed when it was his turn to speak. His mother has decided not to sign Dan up again for the next term. She had been hoping that the extra practice in speech and movement would help him gain in self-esteem and confidence. She was so disappointed! Something else tried and failed! Most parents are so resilient. They never give up for very long: they just withdraw for a while ... to regroup for the next attempt at helping their child become a successful learner.

Dan's mother was talking about this while watching the boys playing soccer one Saturday morning. She is worried about how Dan will manage at school camp. He still wets the bed most nights ... and she is having arguments with him every night lately about not finishing his homework.

Dan's friend, John, explained why he thinks Dan is behaving badly. 'The teacher has said anyone not doing their homework, or completing their work properly, won't be able to go to camp. Dan says he doesn't want to go to the silly old camp anyway, so he won't do his homework. I don't think he has told anyone else about how he still wets the bed. I guess I'd be worried too, if it was me.'

We're waiting, William

William is never ready to begin when everyone else is. He does not have any physical or intellectual impairment that could prevent him from being ready on time. William seems to actually choose to come to each and every task late. It is almost as if he is making a statement by his tardiness. He is a very self-directed child who came to school already able to read. He caused his first year teacher quite a lot of stress through consistently interrupting lessons, often answering questions before they were asked.

William loves to write, and he talks out loud about his writing as he works. He prefers to write when the rest of the class is gathered together for a phonics lesson. He prefers to work on his mathematics worksheets when everyone else is writing. He can be found sitting at the edge of the sandpit putting on his shoes and socks after the lunchbreak, singing happily, while his classmates have all disappeared up the stairs.

Children like William can tend to fray the edges of the most even-tempered teacher. How is it possible to fully include such a child, who is seemingly deliberately intent on exclusive behaviour. Working on the premise that you can't change the child, the only option is to change the teaching practice. By offering a number of options within the structure of the curriculum and the timetable, it would be possible to allow William to indulge his need for making his own choices. All the options are planned by the teacher, and all need to be completed at some time, so eventually, the need to debate the issue of where, when and how will become unnecessary. Through such flexibility, William is satisfied that he is making his own choices, the work will be completed, and most probably a good deal more will be achieved as the child is able to direct creative thinking energy towards the actual learning tasks rather than fretting about who is controlling the situation.

Stories from the playground

Inclusive school playgrounds seem to be quite difficult to establish, as children are participating in activities of their own making, rather than following the directions of a class teacher. Those of us familiar with the many dilemmas of play supervision can understand how some children will present with special needs during playtime. Indeed, the playground is where the success of inclusive philosophy is truly measured.

These stories about lunchtime and playtime are included to illustrate how teaching for inclusion extends beyond the classroom door. Mrs B. relates her experience in a school where special needs children had been supported by a special unit, and educated separately from the rest of the school. They were involved in classes with their age peers for only parts of each day, for what we call the 'soft options' (art, music, religion). These children were known as the 'unit kids'. This situation had existed for many years when Mrs B. was transferred in as the 'unit teacher'. She could feel that these children were not really part of the school. They were students who didn't really have a peer group ... did not really belong. The journey from segregation to being accepted members of classes took two years, but when the third school year started, no one was referred to as 'one of the unit kids'.

Mrs B. spent a great deal of time in the playground during the first eighteen months. Because they ate more slowly, the 'special kids' usually ended up sitting around with the teacher and her assistant, and by the time they finished eating, all the other children were out in the playground, with teams or groups organised. Games were already well in progress. It was rather difficult for anyone to join in then, so the children were at a double disadvantage. They were late arrivals and their games skills were generally poor.

Learning to play

Noticing there seemed to be no imaginative games being played by the special children, Mrs B. decided to begin teaching them how to play. The playground offered great opportunities such as shady trees, an adventure playground, a sandpit, a large well-grassed oval and concrete areas for ball games. The library was open too, for reading, board games or computer play.

Mrs B. realised that these children really did not know how to join in. Many of the children had, for quite significant periods of time, been involved in one-to-one or small group therapy situations. This had caused many 'play' habits which were not particularly peer group appropriate; for example, they found sharing and taking turns difficult. Mrs B. talked this problem over with her colleagues, and plans were made to specifically teach these social interaction skills through cooperative teams.This worked well, and it became evident in the playground that transfer of skills learned in the classroom was occurring. Teachers continued to monitor the playground.

The next step was to directly intervene and 'teach' some games, to develop more participative play patterns. Attention was often drawn to the play of others: 'Look what those kids are playing over there ... that looks like fun! Perhaps we could play a game like that.' Some of the children were quite territorial about where they felt secure in the playground. Anna and Carmel, for instance, tended to spend all their playtime seated on a low brick wall at the back of the school building. It seemed they felt safe there, but they certainly weren't getting much exercise. The teacher played games like 'we're going camping' or 'we're going to the beach', or 'let's play in our castle today!' The language for all these games was modelled by the teacher, so the children learned what would be suitable to say, in the context of the game.

Other children joined in because the games were fun. Gradually, Mrs B. stepped back, perhaps getting the game started, then leaving to watch from a distance. After several weeks, the children had developed enough skills to decide for themselves what they would play, inventing games like 'baby-sitting' and 'going out for lunch'. It was great to hear them planning ahead, thinking up new ideas, sometimes whispering in class, just like everyone else.

Working together

Much of the awkwardness of playtime can be diminished if we are prepared to make the extra effort to include children who have difficulty socialising appropriately. But even allowing for that, even after awareness has been raised and other children are obviously making efforts to adapt their games to suit their different classmates, the special needs can be such that a child may find joining in quite distressing. Or Melinda, who has extreme visual motor integration deficits and cannot cope with playing games involving rules and running, like softball or netball, games that she would dearly love to play. When others are cheering her on, and calling out encouragingly what to do next, she becomes confused, cries, gives up and says 'I can't! I don't know what to do!' She cannot process all the messages and make her body do what it needs to do in such a hurry, and usually ends up in a crumpled heap.

Mrs B. worked with Melinda's classmates, and modelled ways to encourage her without overloading. The children were concerned that they seemed to be causing Melinda such anxiety. One day in the playground, Mrs B. listened to a group of students encouraging Melinda as they played baseball. So very patiently, they were explaining that it was her turn to bat, after two more people, and that she should remember to drop the bat before she ran, and that yes, she did have to run to first base first, even though her best friend was fielding at second base ... Things seemed to be going well, but then Melinda threw herself on the grass crying because it just wasn't fair that she had to go to first base. 'I need to be with my friend,' she cried.

Mrs B. quietly commended the other students for their persistent efforts and suggested they carry on with the game. Taking Melinda by the hand, she spoke comfortingly to her and walked about until the child had regained her equilibrium. The confusion experienced by Melinda makes it hard for her to maintain playtime friendships and she experiences a great deal of emotional upset. Data is presently being collected by the school team about the social situations that seem to cause her most distress. An appropriate social skills program will be developed by the support teacher, class teachers and speech therapist to help the child cope more comfortably with peer interactions.

Even after all this intervention, it can still happen that groups of special needs students will choose to share their playtime. We can explain this by understanding that each of us usually chooses to spend our free time with people or friends with whom we feel most comfortable. We can dream of a school community where nobody minds if their team loses because the child with apraxia, a disorder of the central nervous system, keeps dropping the ball or the child with ataxia, lack of muscular coordination, takes too long to run and place the beanbag in the hoop. We dream and hope ... but for now it's okay that groups of special needs students choose to play together.

Together or alone time

It is important for teachers and other staff to step back from being overprotective and always being around to sort out disagreements. Watching from a distance can often allow a more balanced view of what is actually going on. Most children need some time to be quiet away from peers and active play. Not every child needs to play all the time. Some children tend to cling to the playground supervisor, and need to be encouraged to wander about independently for at least some of the time. While they are with you though, it is a good idea to model the type of language you would want the 'loners' to eventually develop such as 'That looks like a good game', 'What are you playing?', 'Please tell me how to play that game', 'May I join in?', 'I'd like to play that too.'

Although we can all choose to spend some time by ourselves, it seems that children often play alone because they just don't have the appropriate communication skills to ask to join in. We would suggest that there are many resources available to help you develop the social skills program your class needs. Educational bookstores and school suppliers will be able to help. A speech therapist will be able to advise you on more specific skills. You know how you want your class to speak, work and play together. Time invested in teaching and modelling social skills with your students is time invested in an inclusive school and play environment. This is definitely a quality long-term investment.

Social skills

Children who are challenged either intellectually or physically can often have associated social, emotional and communication disorders as well. It can be necessary to teach a class or inform a school community about why certain children do the things they do, or talk the way they talk.

We have found this helps understanding and acceptance of difference. Instead of looking embarrassed or turning away, everyone knows exactly what the problem is, and is able to respond positively. This is reassuring to the special needs students and contributes to their sense of belonging.

Social skills programs are enjoyable, with teachers and students learning more about each other, and from each other. Evidence that they really work is seen and heard at all times during the school day.

Year 6/7 are working in groups ...

Adam: Mrs B., Anna is supposed to be in our group but she won't join in.

Paul: Yes, she won't share the books. There's a whole pile of different books here. She's not using them the way she should, but she won't let us use them either.

Becky: She's cranky now — she's walked off over there by herself.

Mrs B: You know that Anna has great difficulties with understanding what needs to be done ...

Students: Yes, we know that ...

Mrs B: Perhaps if you gave Anna a part of the task to do, something you know she would feel comfortable with ... she needs to feel that you need her in the group.

Becky: I know! She's good at dictionary skills. There's a lot of new words here that we have to find the meanings of.

Paul: Okay, we'll ask Anna to look up the words for us ... and I'll write them down. We'll get through it faster that way.

Adam: Becky and I can answer some of these other questions. Then, we'll talk about what we found out. We should get finished by bell time.

Paul: Oh, Anna! Could you please bring that big dictionary over to our table? We need you to look up some words for us!

Anna's frown changed to a smile. 'Oh sure, Paul. I can do that.'

Mrs B. left them to it. She looked over a few minutes later and made eye contact with Paul, as he waited for Anna to find the next word. He smiled happily, then went on with writing down what Anna told him.

During the lunch break next day, Mrs B. heard evidence of communication skills transfer.

Becky: Come on, Anna, you can join in!

Anna: No, I can't play. I don't want to play with you.

Becky: Don't worry about catching the ball. We need someone to bring the ball back if it goes out of the court. Can you help us?

Anna: Oh yes! I can do that!

The value of role play

To practise 'how to' handle 'tricky situations', the development of skills in role play gives students, and their teachers, a valuable strategy through which they can learn to do their own problem-solving. Role play is useful in helping children understand differences, limitations and needs. People learn in different ways so not everyone can learn appropriate social skills by being told, or by reading, or by completing a worksheet. Powerful learning happens through experience, so role-play activities, carefully planned and facilitated, will be excellent preparation for dealing with the awkward behavioural situations that can frequently come about with special needs students. We have observed remarkable improvements in classes or groups where social skills programs have been enhanced by role play. Everyone benefits!

Obsessions and rituals

Felicity stood watching from the staffroom window which gave an expansive view of the playground. She was observing Jordan as he moved from place to place. This window-gazing was providing interesting information about Jordan's playtime rituals. Jordan has autism and, although he is included in a first year class in a small school, there have been some difficulties with him settling in. This is the sixth week of school and it has taken this long to encourage him to venture out into the playground with the other children. He shows signs of experiencing extreme stress at some times of the day: parting from his mother, moving into or to different parts of the school building, participating with other children in groups. He is even able to vomit at will, which seems to be a way of saying 'This is really stressful for me. I don't want to do this!'

Staff have sought the advice of the Autistic Association. Their education consultant has confirmed that Jordan is indeed indicating that he is feeling uncomfortable, and advised the teachers to allow for obsessional behaviours, to help him feel more secure within the school setting. There are a range of these ritualistic patterns. Jordan has a number of fixed routines: he walks along the corridor touching the same parts of the wall in the same order, saying the same things about the same pictures each time, he eats the same food items for lunch every day, in the same sequence. He prefers dry food, such as crackers and potato crisps. He has perfect manners and follows all the rules about where to sit, eats quietly, then packs his lunchbox away without being reminded. He becomes quite agitated if there is any change to routine events, like when his mother came to work at the tuckshop for the first time. It is not unusual for him to begin crying, seemingly when all the action around him becomes too much to handle.

In the first year class, Jordan is receiving a thorough grounding in early phonics, reading and mathematics. He is withdrawn from the class for occupational and speech therapy sessions. He has strong support from older students, too, who are very understanding of his different behaviour. The support teacher has talked with them about autism. Even though staff often express their own fears that they may not be achieving as much as they would like to with Jordan, the progress, in small steps, even a whispered response in a group activity, or a tentative smile, is encouragement enough to keep on trying.

Who can I call my friend?

Megan sat by herself on the low brick wall around the palm garden, sobbing loudly. As concerned schoolmates hurried over to enquire what was the matter, they were told, 'Go away. Leave me alone! I don't like you!'

This was not the first time Megan had spoken so rudely to them, so the children, knowing that Megan was likely to continue her sobbing for quite a while, came to find the teacher on playground supervision.

'Thank you for telling me,' said Mrs B. 'You go on and play. I'll wander over to talk with Megan. I suspect she has been too bossy with Susie again, and Susie has told her she won't play with her today.'

'Okay!' said the children. 'We'll leave it to you, Mrs B.'

They walked away, but with backward glances towards the unhappy Megan.

Mrs B. smiled. 'It's great to see their genuine concern for Megan. They really don't like to see her get so upset,' she thought to herself.

Megan has epilepsy which had caused her to be in hospital quite a lot when she was younger. The behavioural psychologist suggests that Megan's need to control and dominate her playmates could stem from the fact that so much just happened to her: hospital procedures, medication, scans, and tests of all sorts. She had no control over any of these things, or over the people who were doing them. In any situation where she feels confused, she reacts by giving orders, being bossy, demanding that the rules change to suit her. If others don't comply, first come the tears, then the sobbing.

Megan experiences gross and fine motor difficulties. Her visual motor integration skills are in the lowest 2 per cent of the population. She has certain obsessions, like always carrying her blue pencil case (and there are several others in her desk). She demonstrates very different perceptions of how the world works, yet she can explain in perfect sequence how to drive a car.

It is difficult to be friends with someone like Megan. In fact, it's extremely frustrating. So we believe that other students need to be taught to speak and act in a friendly manner, modelling to Megan a more appropriate way to deal with her anger. We cannot say to students, 'You must be Megan's friend.' That's asking far too much. But we can model how to get along with Megan, explicitly explaining words, phrases and actions that will show Megan we are kind and friendly:

'If you don't like the way we are playing this game perhaps you could play somewhere else.'

'You're welcome to join in — these are the rules …'

'We all take turns at being the leader — it's not your turn just now!'

'You're looking sad today. Can I help?'

2 What is inclusion?

Setting a context

Special needs children are those whose learning needs are usually beyond the training and prior working experience of many classroom teachers and administrators. We have usually labelled such children medically or psychologically, with conditions or names such as Down's syndrome, spina bifida, cerebral palsy or attention deficit disorder.

Not so long ago in Australia, children with mild to extreme special needs were almost always found in institutions and rarely seen in public. Often they were the subject of ridicule and misunderstanding. They had few if any rights and responsibilities. Their capacities were underestimated and they were not seen as fully human with their own dignity and personhood.

In the 1970s there was an increasingly strong movement to 'mainstream' such children into 'normal' situations, including half-way homes and part or whole exposure to education. This was frequently associated with 'special units' located nearby or as part of a school site. The level of communication and involvement of the school with the unit was usually limited. Somewhat similarly in the United States Public Law 94–142 was enacted in 1975 'mainstreaming' special needs children.

During the 1980s this trend gained even more momentum in Australia as parents, in particular, demanded educational provision for their children. There was an expectation, albeit conditional on the part of the school community, that children with special needs had the right to be educated in a classroom with their peers. Economic arguments put forward said this was a less expensive option for educational systems.

Integration

To assist in the integration process, specialist teachers who had been trained in the learning needs and conditions of special needs children acted as tutors and consultants to teachers, helping with program design and frequently withdrawing the child for intervention. What was often lacking was ongoing training and personal support for teachers; by and large, preservice training was quite inadequate for dealing with the realities. Most teachers approached the teaching needs of these children as quite separate from those of other children in the class, and the task of providing for them was often lonely, time consuming and lacking in resources.

In the late 1980s, there were two major changes in special education. Firstly, there was a general change across the country to lowering the IQ standard for admission of children to regular schools. This was as much economically as educationally driven. Secondly, there was increased pressure from a social justice perspective to recognise that all children had the right to an education. This meant an education that was not discriminatory — one that **included** a child with special needs.

There was a shift to recognising the humanity and the personal needs of all special needs children and providing an education that went beyond integration towards acceptance as a member of a learning community. In one sense, educators recognised that full integration of special needs children would only be achieved when inclusion happened first.

Inclusion

One of the most powerful forces behind the move to inclusion has come from those directly involved. Adults with special needs have become advocates for their own rights. Parents have become positively engaged in their children's education, and a large number of support groups have helped to develop community awareness and understanding. In Australia, the Year of the Handicapped raised the profile and highlighted the needs of people with 'disabilities'.

Recently, significant media attention has also been given to competitions such as the Paralympics and other sporting events. The increased profile has also provided a more informed society — at least in terms of recognising that special needs exist and that those with special needs are capable of a great many things.

Educational changes have also been brought about by increased emphasis on socially just teaching strategies and the right of all people to have access to education. For too long schools, as preservers and creators of society, have knowingly or unknowingly created learning situations that have excluded minority groups. Enrolment policies, jargonistic language, physical structures, limited curriculum, information access and teaching methodologies have often shut out some members of our society.

Inclusive classrooms are about the complete range of planned and unplanned experiences that take in knowledge, skills and processes both within the school setting and beyond. They incorporate beliefs about teaching and learning, values, behaviour and ethics. Teachers who fail to recognise this wider context for learning can easily exclude children whose learning needs go beyond the 'normal' range.

The inclusive classroom

Inclusion is about creating a classroom environment that welcomes and values diversity. It challenges all those involved to go beyond what is accepted practice, and to question why exclusion, prejudice and discrimination exist. It aims to build communities of care and acceptance in which the special needs child is no longer different, because all children are valued. It is their right and it is what we all would want for ourselves — to have access to learning in a safe and welcoming environment, free from discrimination and prejudice.

This does not mean that a special needs child cannot be educated apart from his or her peers where appropriate, or where specialist intervention is required; for example, during a visit from an occupational therapist, which in the United States would take place in the regular classroom.

Principles of inclusion

The inclusive classroom is based on rights, learning and relationships. Mara Sapon-Shevin (1991) argues that all children have the right:

- to learn with their age peers

- to be engaged in learning that is appropriate to their skills and needs

- to learn in heterogeneous groups as part of social learning

To these, we would add the following, and they will be critical to the teaching and learning processes developed in this book:

- teachers are facilitators of learning, not just givers of knowledge

- all children have gifts and their diversity enriches both learning and teaching

- authentic learning requires a positive self-esteem

- all children have the right to learn in a safe and welcoming environment

- parents of special needs children have a unique knowledge of, and deep commitment to, the education of their children

- educating special needs children is mutually beneficial for all concerned
- support must be provided

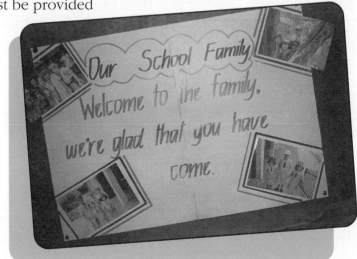

Taking a wider view

Part of developing a fully inclusive classroom is recognising that many of the inhibitions, reservations or difficulties people have with working with special needs children are the result of unchallenged values, practices and situations. Let us take Matthew and Jane as examples.

Matthew has a visual impairment and has difficulty negotiating the steps that lead up to the school library. He loved to use the library, but would not go there on his own. His teacher thought he would not use the library because he was self-conscious about his eyesight. Matthew was actually afraid of falling. The teacher felt he was not prepared to work independently, and discussed the problem with Matthew's parents. The real issues emerged in the discussion. So bright strips were painted on the edges of all the steps and Matthew now spends large amounts of time looking up his favourite topic — dinosaurs.

Jane uses a wheelchair and must travel to her classroom on the second floor via a Stairmate (a mechanical stair-climbing device). On Tuesdays, her class has swimming. The girls go to their classroom to change and then go back to the pool. Everyone complained that by the time Jane got up and down in the Stairmate she had lost almost half her swimming period. Because it was school policy that the children change in their classrooms, no one had thought to allow her to change downstairs.

The benefits

One of our principles of inclusion is that it can be mutually beneficial for all concerned when special needs children are educated as part of so-called regular classrooms. This is supported by research into mixed age grouping which finds that social as well as academic benefits occur when there is a wider than normal range of acceptable behaviours, performances and maturity levels in a classroom. Self-esteem is enhanced, for there are more ways of being accepted and more notions of what is valued.

If everyone brings to the group a commitment to give and to help others to learn, then each person receives much more in return. Children can also learn more about themselves by understanding and valuing the diversity within their own classrooms than they can by seeing those differences as barriers. This is what we refer to as **reciprocity**.

Peer tutoring is frequently used to help special needs learners; their peers must understand very well any material they are working with and new and varied applications are often required by the tutor. This lateral form of development is particularly beneficial to the tutor. And it has leadership, caring and modelling attributes as well.

Another advantage of peer involvement is to do with what is often referred to as **proximal development**. In other words, in some situations, children acting as tutors are often closer to the understandings and needs of their peers than are the teachers. This can be beneficial for the child with special needs and also for the teacher. Having a peer tutor with an understanding of where their classmate is at in relation to learning is a genuine bonus for all. Teachers would evaluate the benefits and appropriateness of peer tutoring according to need, context, subject material and the competencies of the tutor.

Another important skill that is integral to and arises from the education of a special needs child in a classroom is that of **nurturing**. This is not to be confused with sympathy or smothering. Nurturing involves those skills that parents need to care for their own children. It recognises rights, responsibilities and care for those in need. It is patience with understanding — and can be seen where a sighted child assists a visually impaired child with their reading skills or where a teacher takes a step back and waits for a child with limited hand grasp to have a try at picking up his book by himself first.

An inclusive classroom offers an opportunity for children to:

- consider a wider view of the world, and to understand and accept differences

- contribute to the educational endeavours, and to receive from the gifts and talents of others

- contribute positively to physical, social and emotional needs of others

- challenge and change behaviours and beliefs that discriminate against the less fortunate or less powerful in society

The essential elements

What are the essential elements for successfully implementing and maintaining inclusive classrooms. We believe they are:

- a positive attitude

- a commitment to inclusion and inclusive practices

- appropriate skills and knowledge

All these factors are important and interrelated but are dependent upon the underlying attitudes, commitment, past experience and knowledge. The following chapter outlines the necessary considerations and preparations if we are to successfully build and maintain inclusive classrooms.

Creating an inclusive learning environment

The inclusive processes outlined in this chapter are typical of good teaching practice in general. They are signs of a genuine concern for the children that they teach and are based upon certain core beliefs. These signposts are not peculiar to teachers of special needs children but are the link in all good teaching and learning processes.

Building blocks of inclusion

The inclusive classroom is made up of a wide range of interrelating people and issues, all influenced by particular experiences, beliefs and attitudes. These are summarised in figure 3.1.

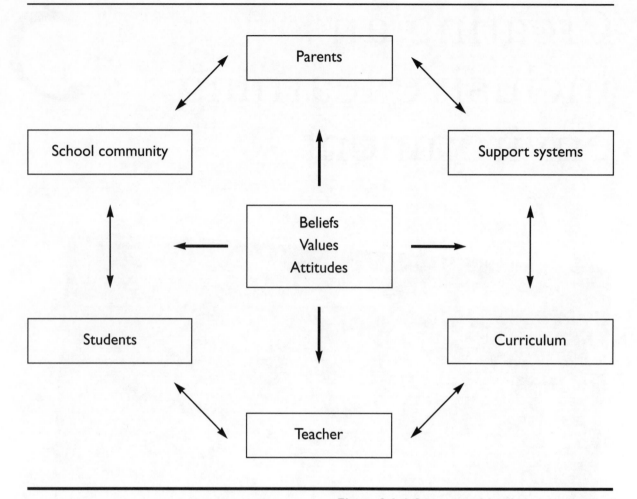

Figure 3.1 Influences on the inclusive classroom ▲

The core of inclusion

The critical element in building a successful inclusive classroom is an appreciation of the integrity of each child, based on the notions of concern, respect and interdependence. Some call it social consciousness and others a love of children. Whatever we call it, there is a strong link between our principles and how we enact our teaching. It is what we truly believe about teaching and learning that will affect the way in which we come to the inclusive classroom, and it is those beliefs or principles that will inform or colour the processes we use.

Figure 3.2 shows that the responsibility for the success of the inclusion process rests primarily with the teacher. It is also important to remember that specialist support, in the form of intervention, might be the area that a teacher can rely upon least in the classroom.

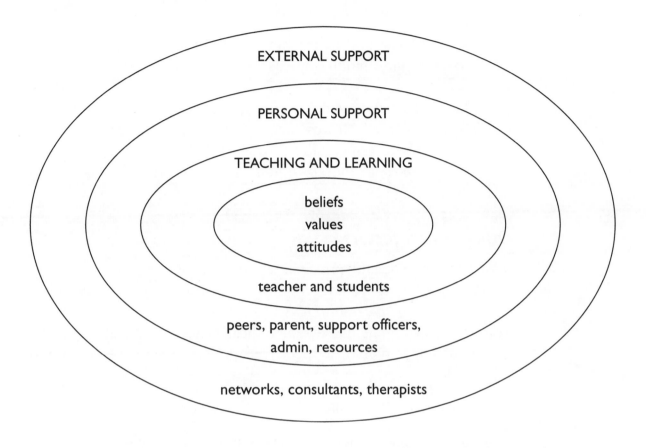

EXTERNAL SUPPORT

PERSONAL SUPPORT

TEACHING AND LEARNING

beliefs

values

attitudes

teacher and students

peers, parent, support officers,
admin, resources

networks, consultants, therapists

Figure 3.2 At the core of inclusion ▲

Teaching and learning

Special needs learners exist within a learning community and as teachers we are there to ensure that they have the best possible opportunities for learning. Teaching special needs children is no different, in one sense, from quality teaching for all children. Consider these points from *Principles of Effective Learning and Teaching* (1994).

1   Effective learning and teaching is founded on an understanding of the learner.

2   Effective learning and teaching requires active construction of meaning.

3   Effective learning and teaching enhances and is enhanced by a challenging environment.

4 Effective learning and teaching is enhanced through worthwhile learning partnerships.

5 Effective learning and teaching shapes and responds to social and cultural contexts.

Inclusive education will succeed if the teacher and the school embrace all the available resources, both human and physical, in a spirit of openness, respect and flexibility. When the principles listed above are enacted in the classroom, they serve to create genuinely inclusive learning.

Other critical factors

What happens when the principal says to a teacher:

Mary you've got 27 kids in your class next year and I'm giving you the boy with cerebral palsy.

This situation highlights several critical factors that will affect the successful integration of a special needs learner into a school and classroom:

- the process of enrolment and individual case evaluation

- advance preparation for teachers and school community

- the attitude of teacher and school to inclusion

These issues are discussed in depth later. Advance preparation is a key component of creating a successful classroom learning environment for all. It would be unfair to suggest that there will be less work for a teacher of a child with special needs, but it is important to recognise that there are ways of maximising the support and the teaching and learning situations to assist.

As well as the usual case evaluations for placement of a special needs child, we strongly recommend that teachers and schools consider some of the following issues as part of the enrolment and preparation process. Reflect on the implications of these questions for yourself and your teaching.

Personal

- Do you have a positive attitude?
- What is your personal commitment?
- Do you have a positive vision for this child's learning?
- Do your personal values flow through to your teaching practice?

Professional

- Does your teaching reflect principles of social justice?
- Do you have appropriate skills and knowledge for teaching children with special needs?
- Do you have access to specialist advice, resources and support?
- Do you have knowledge of inclusive practices and curriculum?

Support systems

- Do you have understanding and supporting peers?
- What frequency of support can you count on?
- Do you plan to use parent involvement in the inclusion process?

Teaching and learning

- What is your understanding of cooperative learning, peer tutoring, mentoring?
- Do you make use of reflection and metacognition?
- Do you teach communication and social skills?
- Are your teaching and learning processes and expectations flexible?
- Have you a variety of relevant strategies for evaluation and assessment?

Your classroom

- Is there flexibility in arrangement, timetabling and lesson structure?
- Is the classroom environment welcoming to children and parents?
- Is diversity recognised, understood and valued?

Figure 3.3 Checklist for teachers of special needs students ▲

Inclusive climates: the classroom environment

The responsibility and the action of inclusion takes place in the classroom, and the inclusive classroom is more easily developed where basic human needs are met. When we create a classroom environment that meets these needs, it greatly increases the chances of children learning in a safe yet challenging setting.

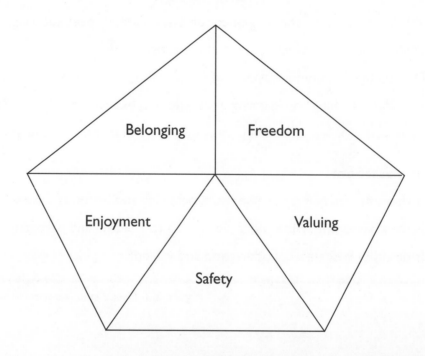

Figure 3.4 The basic needs of children in a learning environment ▲

Belonging

Consider when, as adults, we have faced new and unfamiliar situations. Learning new skills, breaking into established friendships, forming new friendships and learning new routines and procedures are not easy for everyone. Putting down roots and belonging are essential to happiness for each person. William Glasser (1988) describes this as a sense of 'belonging' — that is to love, share and cooperate. Moorman & Dishon (1982) talk of it as a sense of 'rootedness' — a place you belong in and trust. We describe it as meeting our need to have purpose, or having a connection with life and self.

How can we build a classroom that helps the special needs child find a sense of belonging and acceptance? What would it look like? sound like? feel like?

An inclusive learning environment is the one that recognises and meets the social, physical, psychological and intellectual needs of students without favour or prejudice. At its core is the sense of belonging. Skilful teachers will begin by building a sense of class, group and personal belonging. This sense of belonging necessitates acceptance by each of these groups as well. In other words, an inclusive learning environment helps children to see beyond tolerance to acceptance of differences and eventually to valuing the uniqueness of others. In the case of special needs children, this may also mean developing a sense of belonging in the school and in society.

Kagan (1990) identifies five aims of class and team building:

- getting acquainted

- class/team identity building

- experiencing mutual support

- valuing individual differences

- developing synergy

The physical environment

The physical environment gives messages about the sense of welcome and belonging that we as teachers have for our students.

- Does the classroom exhibit warmth in layout, colour, personal spaces, group spaces, lighting and flexibility of arrangement?

- Does it offer children opportunities to find solitude as well as company?

- Are the children encouraged to design and create their own physical environment, based on the values and interests they share and the needs they have?

- What use is made of the children's own personal decorations, art works, alternative materials, parents' skills, and other resources?

The personal classroom

Classrooms are places where children spend a major part of their lives. We often speak of school being like a family. An inclusive classroom is one where children have a sense of belonging and acceptance.

Consider the following simple ways of encouraging positive values and personal involvement on the part of children:

- personal stories, anecdotes, family or child snapshots, birthday calendars and celebrations

- favourite pets, pastimes, colours, class-made books

- getting-to-know-you games

- personal letters from teacher to student, teacher/student journals

- poems, stories, reading, writing based on values such as friendship, love, home, happiness, cooperation

- team and class-building games and activities that stress and teach cooperation, understanding and communication

- other games, activities that examine social issues such as discrimination, rejection or misunderstanding

- team and class names, logos, mottos, songs, raps, charter of rights

These suggested ideas can help teachers to build a classroom where children are more than just aware of their classmates. They have more opportunities to get to know them more personally. Building a sense of belonging requires a commitment to each other and a sense of the worth of each other.

The welcoming classroom

We can give many messages about welcoming and belonging:

- warm open body language

- friendly greetings, interested conversations with students

- taking time to eat, learn, play, laugh together

- positive phrasing free of put-downs or sarcasm

- being approachable and honest

- able to model inclusive practices and challenge exclusive ones

- able to say and mean 'we' and 'us'

The notion of belonging is summed up in this quote from *The Wind in the Willows* where Mole reflects on his unplanned return to his modest home.

It was good to think he had this to come back to, this place that was his own, these things that were so glad to see him again and could always be counted upon for the same simple welcome.

It is important to feel wanted — to feel that if I were away from my class today, it would be noticed and I would be welcomed back tomorrow.

For more information, ideas and programs, we recommend that readers refer to the titles listed in the resources section.

Freedom

'What we want is the freedom to choose how we are to live our lives, to express ourselves freely, associate with whom we choose, read and write what satisfies us, and worship or not worship as we believe.' (Glasser 1986)

In the classroom, this notion of freedom is particularly felt when children express the need to learn according to their preferred styles and modes of learning, with or without others and in areas of interest and ability.

Many of us have experienced rebellious behaviour when children's learning and emotional/social needs have not been met. The same is equally true of special needs children. An inclusive classroom recognises the need for all children to take control over their own lives, as much as possible. Nurturing children's maturity is a task that requires a balance between planned opportunities for free expression and providing social and thinking skills that will help children to make wise choices.

Classrooms where this need is being addressed would be places where:

- children take as much responsibility for their learning
  as possible through:
  - child-developed projects, themes, learning centres
  - personal goal-setting and review
  - individual or group checklists and assessments
  - open-ended problem-solving and enquiry

- children are engaged in social skill development that:
  - enables them to interact appropriately with their peers
  - prepares them for living in society
  - is linked to responsible citizenship
  - allows them to communicate their needs and feelings

- children are engaged in decision-making that:
  - is reflective and seeks acceptable alternatives
  - is real life and life-like
  - recognises the child's capabilities and responsibilities
  - opens the door to new experiences and challenges old ones
  - respects and protects the rights of others

Enjoyment

When we really enjoy something we will persist longer, repeat often, internalise and share with others. Classrooms should be places where having fun is the norm, not the exception. Laughter, enjoyment and fun are examples of our need to make life pleasurable. Children, like adults, enjoy communities where they are free to enjoy each others' company and talents. Enjoyment is like Glasser's (1986) notion of 'fun'. It is that feeling good energy that makes life worthwhile.

We know that quality teaching and learning occurs when self-esteem is high and self-esteem is enhanced when we enjoy doing what we are doing. A classroom that provides challenge with personal responsibility and yet is still a place where students enjoy being and learning is meeting essential criteria for an inclusive classroom.

Children enjoy school and learning when:

- they feel welcome and can identify self with the school

- they feel that they have a contribution to make

- they succeed

- that success is recognised and valued

- they have friends

- they can play

- the teacher can laugh with the children and at themselves

- there is variety in learning approaches and resources

- failure is not seen as failure but as a stepping-stone to new pathways and then success

Valuing

Not too far distant from the notion of belonging is valuing. Valuing is related to self-worth and self-esteem. Developing a classroom that values diversity is the first step in building an inclusive learning community. When we are valued for what we have to offer, it increases our sense of self-worth and this has a reciprocal effect on the quality of our learning and our participation in learning. Consider, for example, the power of celebrating birthdays; everyone has one, everyone can be valued for who they are, no strings, performance, features, qualities attached!

Programs and activities that are used to develop this notion of valuing should promote:

- knowledge and appreciation of self through:
  - recognising one's gifts, abilities and limitations
  - understanding one's needs and goals
  - a supportive and caring community
  - reflection and dialogue

- a community of learners that:
  - values diversity in talents, culture, learning style, gender
  - is sensitive to individual needs
  - involves the wider context, e.g. parents and the whole school
  - encourages 'having a go'
  - uses supportive, positive language skills

Safety

We learn well when there is challenge combined with a supportive learning environment and low stress. Children with special needs, too, need classroom environments that offer challenges which are attainable and realistic. Goal-setting and reflection on learning are important aspects of this process. Safety is like Glasser's (1986) notion of 'survival'. No one takes risks when they are likely to fail dismally or be humiliated because of their inadequacies.

Safety in the inclusive classroom is an essential ingredient for building the sense of belonging. If we are different, we may have to take bigger risks and need more support to do so.

Special needs learners like all children need an emotional safety net. If, on one hand, we know that challenge makes us grow, then to allow risk-taking to occur means that we must provide for failure or clumsiness. If we have created a classroom where there is a sense of belonging, freedom, valuing and enjoyment, then there is a place where risk-taking and challenge can be provided.

Providing a classroom of safety means that:

- children can be who they are and feel comfortable with that

- prejudice and bias are confronted and understood, and perhaps changed

- children are encouraged and rewarded for attempting to go beyond themselves

- there is trust — who I am will not be betrayed or belittled

- communication is positive, conflict is productive

4 Managing the environment

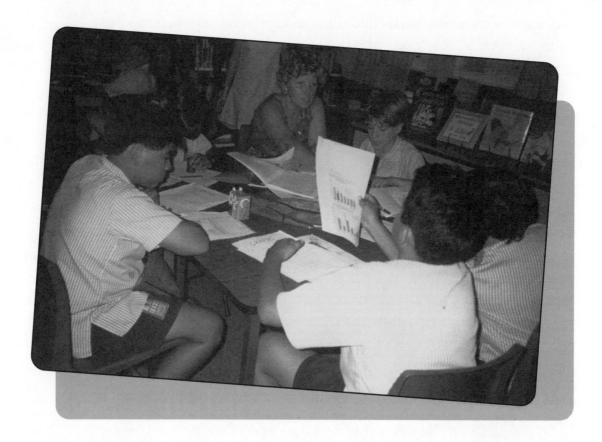

The challenge for teachers of children with limited academic, physical or other abilities is to provide an education that allows them participation in a meaningful and relevant way. Using a variety of strategies, support people and physical resources is usually more successful than simply providing a special program in the same room, or a separate program in another room.

Learning principles

There are certain constants that we must bear in mind if we are to provide the type of quality learning that our children require. If we take the principles of effective learning and teaching mentioned earlier, and look at their implications, then we have a substantial framework for developing appropriate learning structures.

1 Understanding individuals

In nearly all cases, teachers will have considerable information — medical, psychological, social, family, academic and so on — about their special needs learner. Here are some key points for consideration when beginning to focus on appropriate teaching and learning strategies for an individual child:

- the nature of learning difficulties

- the limitations on involvement and expectations

- the child's motivation and self-esteem

- prior experiences and learning to build on

- the child's learning style and interests

- the expectations of parents, teachers and others that limit or extend

- relationships with peers

2 Construction of meaning

Too often in the past, educational programs for special needs children were not relevant in terms of their day-to-day or future life. The challenge is to make learning meaningful for all. This can be accomplished when we provide learning that:

- challenges individuals to grow

- offers a variety of real life and life-like scenarios

- provides variety in learning styles, processes and outcomes

- links prior knowledge to the present and future

- is reflective and linked to goal-setting

- is practical, purposeful and creative

- uses a variety of thinking processes at different levels of complexity

- integrates the home and school learning environments

3 Classroom environment

Characteristics of a quality learning environment that is both challenging and supportive include:

- quality relationships that emphasise caring, belonging and responsiveness

- independence and interdependence

- effective communication between teachers, students and parents

- well-planned and resourced programs

- participation by parents in the learning processes

- cooperation, collaboration and team work

- adaptable programs that provide for different learning rates

- predictable yet flexible timetables and routines

In Kathleen's year 2 classroom a large coloured poster is divided into the days of the week for the daily timetable. The timetable features large written and drawn symbols of the day's activities. Team work time is represented by a drawing of three children holding up a box, individual work is shown as one child reading on the box. The children in the class refer to the timetable after each break to know where they need to be for the next learning session.

Their teams last for about 4 to 6 weeks. They have given their teams names, mottos and badges. They have both team and personal goals to meet. Both Kathleen and the other team members are involved in helping each child to set his or her learning goals.

Kathleen uses parents in the classroom constantly. Her goal is to create a family-type classroom. Feelings are discussed, social and communication skills are discussed and practised. And when good things like birthdays, special events and accomplishments occur the class takes special pride in celebrating these.

Kathleen meets with the children every morning for open discussions and for developing learning programs that are based on the children's interests. She realises that rich learning experiences can sometimes be spontaneous or unplanned and can come from the children's everyday life — like the time James found a snake skin or the time Maria fought with Patric over another friend. She used both of these occasions to develop learning situations that dealt with reptiles and with friendships. Rather than seeing these things as interruptions to her program, she used them to enhance the real-life learning of the children.

4 Learning partnerships

No knowledge was ever created in a vacuum. We learn by learning with or through others. Children whose relationships with others are limited may need specially structured learning to provide for worthwhile interpersonal contact — both academically and socially.

Teachers of special needs children must utilise all their resources and those resources, we believe, are largely people resources. Parents, peers, administrators, teacher aides, therapists, advisers and students are key parts of the learning environment of the special needs child and should be actively involved wherever possible. Consider providing worthwhile learning partnerships by:

- using cooperative learning processes and situations

- providing opportunities to discuss goals and aspirations

- developing regular meetings for reflection, feedback and planning

- encouraging open and frequent communication

- sharing observations and assessment of learning tasks and social interactions

- inviting ideas and suggestions from all members of the learning community

As a result of brain damage during infancy, Lynda has very restricted speech. She is very difficult to understand and uses a variety of hand signs to communicate her basic needs and ideas. Terry, her teacher, invited in her mother, Sue, to work with the class teaching them Lynda's basic sign language. Over a few weeks Lynda's classmates became very adept at signing. New signings were invented by the children to help with their communication with Lynda. The children compiled and printed a signing chart.

Lynda was noticeably pleased by the way in which her classmates took to the signing. They were better able to communicate with her and now had a deeper understanding of the difficulties Lynda faced in communicating with others. Her mother felt that she was able to contribute something positive and useful to Lynda's learning situation as well.

5 Social and cultural contexts

Recognising that special needs learners have rights is only a part answer to helping them integrate into society. The inclusion process necessitates community and classroom education into the nature and effects of a need. Effective classrooms are those that form and respond to social, cultural contexts when they:

- look at, understand and value diversity in their midst

- develop attitudes of acceptance, tolerance and harmony

- reflect on conditions and situations that discriminate against or inhibit people reaching their full potential

- challenge and change practices that are discriminatory

- provide learning strategies that take into account and value the social and cultural contexts of the learners

After a year 7 student experienced a seizure at a friend's house one weekend, the integration support teacher at her school saw the need for education of staff and students about epilepsy. Since there were a number of children in the school who could experience different forms of seizure, teachers and students needed to be aware of what could happen, what it would look like and what to do about it. Using a video from the Epilepsy Association, lessons were planned to suit a range of classes.

Discussions that followed the input prepared children as to how they should react if they saw someone in the playground or community experiencing a seizure.

Management and organisation

Teachers in quality learning environments use a variety of teaching methodologies. Figure 4.1 shows what we believe are essential components of the teaching approaches to be used with students with special learning needs. While they are not all-encompassing, we believe that they have the potential for teachers and students to address the key principles of inclusive learning and teaching.

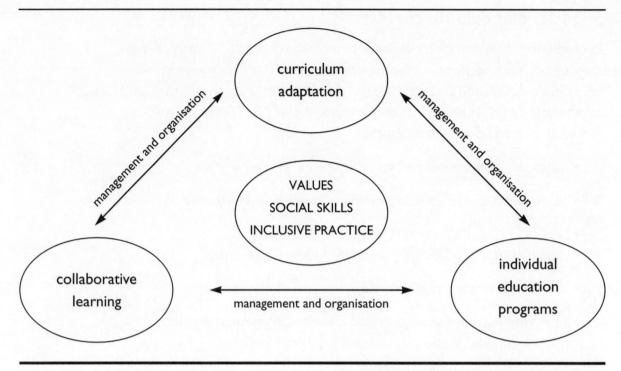

Figure 4.1 Teaching in the inclusive classroom ▲

At the core are teachers' beliefs, values and practices. Binding the pieces together, almost like a glue, are the necessary social skills and classroom management and organisational strategies. Social skills such as listening, turn-taking or praising provide the tools to promote communication and problem-solving. They must be explicitly taught, modelled and used often.

Classroom organisation and management strategies demand professional judgement, planning, experience and flexibility. Consistency, predictability and justice are evident in their implementation.

Effective teaching and learning environments are supported by well-managed classroom communities that enable each child to develop more than just academically. Good management and organisation revolves around a wide range of skills and organisational strengths. Among the most important are the following:

- clarity of goals

- advance planning

- knowledge of individual students and their needs

- a range of behaviour/learning intervention strategies

- consistency

- justice tempered with wisdom

- foresight

- teacher self-confidence and self-esteem

Management and organisation in the inclusive classroom is built around the principles described in Chapter 3 — belonging, freedom, valuing, enjoyment and safety — and these need to be modelled, made explicit, AND practised often.

Some teachers seek to achieve self-managing classrooms where the children assume much of the responsibility for the learning environment, in terms of the management and organisational structures. The children create and develop class norms and rules, even classroom covenants that guarantee their rights and the values they hold dear. The children create the meanings for these norms of behaviour and organisation — they are enabled to take more responsibility for their own participation and actions.

These elements are to be found in good teachers' classrooms, everywhere. They are essential to an inclusive classroom. They help children come to understand that rights exist alongside responsibilities.

Where children can contribute positively to creating and maintaining supportive learning environments, their motivation to participate, to belong and to succeed become more intrinsic. And intrinsically motivated learners learn best!

What aspects of the classroom management and organisation are related to an effective and inclusive teaching and learning environment? The following are some that appear to be inseparable from good teachers' classrooms:

- the physical environment

- covenants, rules and norms

- directions and structures

- student and teacher roles

- recognition of development, growth, achievement

- extension or assistance

The physical environment

How we structure and set up our classrooms says a great deal about:

- what we value about learning

- how we see our relationship to the students

- the place of student interactions

- our pride and their pride in the classroom

- the sense ownership the children have for their learning

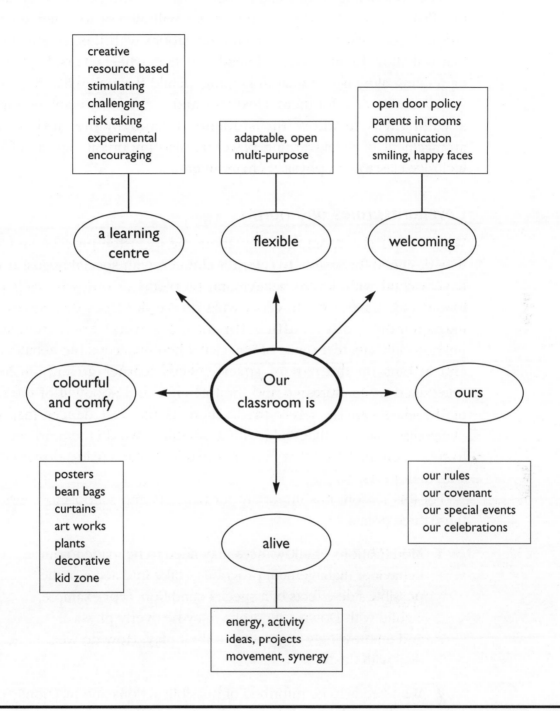

creative
resource based
stimulating
challenging
risk taking
experimental
encouraging

adaptable, open
multi-purpose

open door policy
parents in rooms
communication
smiling, happy faces

a learning
centre

flexible

welcoming

colourful
and comfy

Our
classroom is

ours

posters
bean bags
curtains
art works
plants
decorative
kid zone

alive

our rules
our covenant
our special events
our celebrations

energy, activity
ideas, projects
movement, synergy

Figure 4.2 Our classroom environment ▲

If the physical layout of the inclusive classroom says anything, it should say 'welcome'. The inclusive classroom is a place where there is 'us' and 'we', not 'me' and 'you'. There is a sense of mutual ownership, joint responsibility and belonging for teacher and student.

This welcoming environment (both physical and personal) is often the first sign of the school and class's willingness to integrate the special needs learner. An appealing classroom with flexible structures that will allow for any physical needs (such as wheel chairs, leg braces or walking aids) is essential in helping a child through what may be a very daunting time for them. Flexibility and adaptability combined with a willingness to allow the students a hand in the design and arrangement of their learning place are also important aspects of the inclusive classroom's physical environment.

Covenants, rules and norms

What do our classroom rules say about the inclusion process, and are they designed for or able to cater for children with special needs? If we have a child with severe behavioural problems or one who calls out loudly and aggressively in class, what do we do? Does our behaviour management policy suffice for all occasions? Some teachers unknowingly create a sense of injustice when unacceptable behaviours and actions on the part of special needs learner go unpunished, unrebuked or unaddressed and the tolerance and goodwill of the rest of the class can be sorely tried. There is the real danger that we overcompensate for that child with a disability. We do them no service to treat them in a way that may be prejudicial and creates disharmony with their peers.

For this reason, it is important for teachers and schools to consider these three points:

1 Modifications or allowances may need to be made to our behaviour management program to take into account the possible side-effects of a special condition. (For example, a child with Down's syndrome may be overly physical and unknowingly aggressive in their play. How do we deal with this?)

2 Who needs to be informed of possible actions and reactions from a special needs learner that would affect order, discipline and management? Do school support officers or volunteer parents for example, need to know what might occur if they work with Johnny? How will they deal with swearing or hitting? What support measures are available for time-out for the student and, perhaps, the teacher?

3 Most importantly, has the class been adequately prepared for what they would normally consider unacceptable behaviours? Do we have rules and regulations that apply in all situations? Can we be sure that decisions that we take are:

- fair and equitable for all parties

- based on an understanding of the nature of the learner

- will maintain tolerance and understanding

Rules

Rules are sometimes necessary, though we believe that there are more enabling alternatives such as the covenant and norms listed below. If you choose to have rules consider these 'six rules for rules'.

It is important to point out though, that not all special needs learners present with behavioural or social problems. The inclusive classroom is **just** to all, **respectful** to all and is **open** to the needs of all.

Six rules for rules

1 Keep them simple — long-winded rules are easily forgotten.

2 Let the students create them — they will take more ownership.

3 Write them as positives — positive phrasing encourages.

4 Have as few rules as possible — less to remember.

5 Be realistic — be sensitive to age, maturity and needs.

6 Review them often — remove unnecessary ones, add relevant ones.

Covenants

A covenant (Kagan 1990) is an agreement. In the classroom setting it might be an agreement on a set of beliefs about how we wish to be treated or valued in a classroom. The advantage of a covenant over a set of class rules is that it sets a framework for addressing the many issues outside the scope of normal classroom rules. The following example was developed by a year 5 class in their first week of school.

> **In Sunshine Class**
>
> We have the right to be safe, happy and able to learn.
>
> We agree to work together.
>
> We agree to share our gifts, talents and ideas.
>
> We agree to give help when it is asked, with a smile.
>
> We agree to solve problems so that everyone wins.
>
> We agree to speak and act so that we are safe, happy and able to learn.

When the class got together in the first week, the teacher led the children through some experiences and reflections on school and living with other people. They looked at what made them happy at school and what helped them to learn well. Groups brainstormed ideas and thoughts. They classified these into headings and agreed on what were the most important things they wanted to see in their classroom. Above all, they wanted a classroom where they would be safe, happy and able to learn.

The teacher led them on to a process where they looked at what it would be like to have such a classroom. They described a classroom with no bullying, put-downs, fighting or aggression. She turned it around to ask what would you see, hear and feel. They described their classroom as one where respect was shown through using first names, 'please', 'thank you', and so on.

The important thing to highlight here is that she got them to describe the signs of the classroom covenant being enacted. These signs became the skills and values that they actively pursued in their cooperative learning classes. They have no class rules. Every issue that arises is dealt with in terms of the covenant.

Norms

Norms (Kagan 1990) are more explicit than the classroom covenant. They describe the behaviours and expectations of individuals, groups, or people in roles within groups. Norms have the advantage of describing clearly what the expectations in a certain situation are. Some children with very poor social and interpersonal skills need explicit information as to their participation and interactions with others. Consider the following class norms.

In our classroom

I am responsible for:

Me	*my* desk, books, materials, loans, assignments, homework
Learning	participating, listening, staying on task, completing tasks
Asking	think first, explore ideas, get other opinions
Helping	encouraging, supporting, smiling, praising, listening

We are responsible for:

Us	*our* room, library, materials, projects, happiness
Learning	sharing work and ideas, participating, finishing
Asking	seeking other people's ideas, help and skills
Helping	assisting, encouraging, welcoming, other groups

The advantage in using a norms type approach is that it defines the expected behaviours and procedures so that ambiguity is removed and the values of the classroom are reinforced in a visible and clear manner. The added advantage of class-developed norms is that the students have identified what they consider important and the commitment to living by the norms of the class is likely to be higher than to teacher-developed rules.

Giving directions

It is not unusual for a teacher of a special needs learner to use a wider range of strategies for communicating directions and structures. For example, teachers can make use of the student's peers for communicating some signals, or board work for a visually impaired child. Similarly, the use of a nonverbal no-noise signal, might be important when teaching a child with significant hearing loss.

For the wide range of exceptionality possible in a classroom, there are a host of simple adaptations that can be made. Discussing these with a specialist, a visiting teacher or an advocate from a support group is often the best way to reduce minor frustrations and increase effective teaching time.

Consider the following when working with special needs learners:

1 Directions should be simple and clear. Employ a number of modes of conveying the message. Use a mentor or team-mate as a clarifier for the child.

2 Break the task or instruction down into the smallest parts. Let each part be achieved in turn. Recognise the success of each part being achieved or accomplished.

3 Check for understanding and perception often. We cannot always assume that the child has the process or directions clearly in their mind. Sometimes the slightest thing out of routine can cause major dramas.

4 Practise and model. Have the student practise the skills separately if necessary. Model the behaviours, skills and steps yourself, or perhaps have other students model them. Recognise and reward effort and accomplishment.

Recognition

Everyone desires some recognition of development, growth or achievement, and special needs learners are no different. Care needs to be taken that praise is not effusive or over-the-top because of the child's physical, intellectual or emotional needs. Children easily detect condescending behaviour — it stifles positive relationships and increases self-doubt on the part of the child. The sense of being valued relates very well to what reward/recognition systems and processes we use in the classroom.

When we consider building an inclusive classroom where special needs learners are as much a part of the classroom culture as any other child do we:

- build attitudes of pride and pleasure in each other's growth and achievements?

- enable children to recognise and be proud of their own development or achievements?

- teach children appropriate ways of praising and recognising effort, change and achievement?

- help children deal with lack of success or failure, and encourage them to keep persisting?

- value some skills or abilities more than others? Are we open to all types of endeavour — recognising that while they may not be valued by us, they might be a great source of pride to the students?

- build on student interests to promote understanding and valuing of diversity — especially getting to know each other beyond school?

Special needs learners, like any other students, require reinforcement, recognition and personal skills for dealing with challenges. Some of those challenges might require far more persistence and perseverance than the average student needs to accomplish the task.

And though there is increased legal awareness these days, we advocate strongly for the need for touch. Many special needs learners are acutely aware that some people find it difficult to relate to them by way of touch. A hug, a pat or a high five are extremely important signs of being valued or congratulated or consoled.

Extension

Extend special needs learners? Absolutely! We need challenge to make us grow. Challenges should be based on our interests, needs and capacities. There is no reason why the extension type programs or activities teachers provide for their 'normal' class cannot be available for special needs learners. Perhaps more capable students could develop extension activities or make materials, games and learning centres. We encourage them to think of another's learning needs — another person's welfare. We encourage and facilitate a community of learners in cooperation.

5 Strategies for teaching and learning

Collaborative learning

Not only do we gain enormously from the social interactions and modelling of behaviours and skills, but we are open to many more ideas and problem-solving possibilities when we work with others. Special needs learners are the same: they, more than other learners, need to encounter as many learning and social situations as possible to develop their potential skills.

When a child enters the classroom, there are several collaborative learning approaches that involve students learning with, from and beside other people. These may involve team-mates, peer tutors or adults in a mentoring role. A brief examination of the scope and potential of each model follows.

Cooperative learning

There is significant research that demonstrates the benefits of cooperative learning models — especially for special needs learners. Cooperative learning is both a method of learning with others and also a philosophy that values the social and personal benefits of living and learning with others. It is used as a methodology and as a teaching ethic. Among the benefits for special needs learners are the valuing of diversity and the understanding of differences that is developed through cooperative learning.

The benefits

The benefits of cooperative learning taken from research are summarised below (Moorman 1993). We have categorised these benefits into four major areas: affective, attitudinal, social and cognitive.

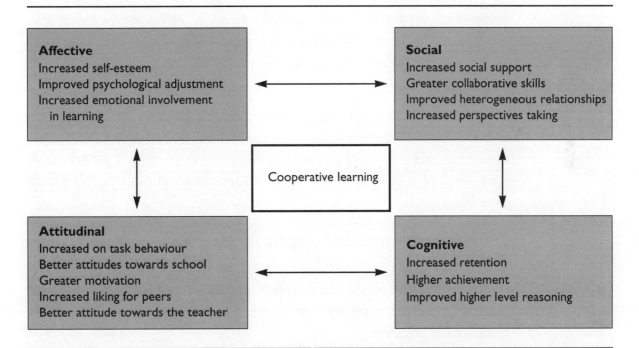

Figure 5.1 The benefits of cooperative learning (adapted from a summary of research by Moorman 1993) ▲

Among the findings of research into cooperative learning highlighted by Moorman are several that have enormous implications for the development of an inclusive classroom. The following outcomes or benefits should encourage all teachers of special needs learners to consider cooperative learning as a teaching and learning strategy.

Affective

Self-esteem and self-acceptance are two benefits of cooperative learning. Emotional maturity is fostered because of the focus on independence and interdependence rather than dependence. Respect, courtesy and social skills are developed.

Attitudinal

Research shows better attitudes towards school, peers and teachers where cooperative learning is used frequently. There is more tolerance of difference and appreciation of the uniqueness of each other. Motivation moves from extrinsic to intrinsic and perseverance increases. The quality of the interactions is superior to traditional models of teaching.

Social

In the social area, cooperative learning highlights the positive valuing of difference and the integration of students with special needs. A wider range of friendships develop and a sense of belonging is developed. More collaboration and cooperation occurs in a classroom where a wider range of opinions and views are encouraged.

Cognitive

There is more on-task, higher level thinking, problem-solving and learning in a cooperative learning classroom. There is modelling and encouragement of critical thinking skills, and increased retention of ideas and concepts because of the wider range of learning situations possible.

The essential elements of cooperative learning

There are many excellent resources for understanding and implementing the cooperative learning approach, and there are several listed in the reference section. What follows is a basic overview of cooperative learning.

Johnson and Johnson (1985) state that there are five key elements of cooperative learning. These elements are necessary for the learning partnerships to be effective, both academically and socially.

Face-to-face learning

Learning takes place with others. Teachers need to structure team learning so that there is interaction. This means that social, communication and negotiation skills are developed and utilised.

Mary has set up today's learning in pairs. Each child will read the same item from the paper and then write responses to set questions on their own sheet of paper. In turn, they will give their answers to their team-mate. If they differ in their answers they must discuss it until they agree on an answer. If they cannot come to a common answer, they may ask another group for help when they have completed all the other questions.

When they are satisfied that they have all the correct answers, they sign each other's papers and hand them in to the teacher. The emphasis is on discussion, giving help and reaching consensus. Mary discussed and gave examples of these processes in action before the task began. The children then had a model to use.

Positive interdependence

By having common goals, shared resources, roles that relate to the task of the group, team names, one outcome or a shared work space, we can focus children on working cooperatively together to achieve *our* product. Where groups strive to include all members, there is greater productivity and cognition.

Christine, James and Micha are solving a mapping problem together. They have one map, one set of questions and one pen to use at one desk. Because of the limited space and materials, the chances of their working together are increased. When they finish, they all sign their names to the product indicating agreement and joint ownership. Sometimes their teacher asks the children to take on specific roles within their groups, such as recorder, researcher or reporter. In this way she develops particular skills and forces the children to interact with each other to achieve their goal.

Since Micha has very poor muscle tone and control in her arms and hands, she takes on roles in her group that are within the scope of her abilities. At times, her involvement may be modified. She might not write responses but record them on tape. She is helped by her peers when pages need to be turned or reports held up for display. In fact, Micha's teacher often asks the group to modify the roles so that Micha has a meaningful part to play in the learning activity.

Individual accountability

Everyone is expected to contribute to a group. The contribution may be modified if necessary. No one is allowed to hitchhike or piggyback on the work others. It is possible to make sure that each child takes responsibility for learning and making sure others in the group understand and participate.

In Brenda's classroom the children are working on a science project. She wants each child to cover all the concepts but there are too many for detailed study. Each group then has four science concepts for study. They decide who will specialise in an area. They split up to study and research their topic. They are to hand in to the teacher a detailed response on their chosen topic. In their groups though, they present a shortened version which includes major points and ideas. Their team-mates listen and complete their own personal summary sheet of each presenter in their group. These summary sheets are collected by the teacher.

In this way Brenda has enabled each child to have a choice in their specialist study area but they are also compelled to complete a summary sheet which will be collected and assessed. While they learn from each other, they are still responsible for handing in their own materials. The team structure in this situation helps the children to develop both independence and interdependence. As well as this, the team members each complete a summary sheet of information they received from their team-mates' specialised feedback to the group.

Interpersonal/social skills

Many group learning experiences have failed because teachers have not taught or made explicit what social skills would be needed in the activity and what they would look or sound like. Children need interpersonal skills for good communication and problem-solving as well as group maintenance skills such as affirming, including and inviting participation.

> Today in year 6, the children are working in pairs to complete a mapping exercise. One child has a map without towns or other names but with coordinates. The other child has the complete set of information in their atlas. The child with the map must ask questions of their partner to help complete the tasks set by Kym, their teacher, and the other responds with information. After the sheet is complete they compare. There is discussion and celebration when the activity is completed and compared.
>
> The activity will need the children to be actively listening, questioning and clarifying information. Their class teacher has spent the last two weeks highlighting what these skills would look like and sound like in action. She has drawn up sample questions on large sheets of paper and placed them at the front of the room. It is not unusual to see a child look up at the questioning skills chart for ideas on how to frame a question or clarify information from their partner.

Reflection

There are many excellent resources available now to assist teachers and team members to identify both the interpersonal and subject content of their group work. Reflection is an ideal process for setting goals for future work, analysing past efforts and tackling personal or group commitment. It is the beginning point for children to engage in meta-cognitive processing of learning and a key learning skill.

> In Kym's classroom, the children have completed their mapping task. Now Kym asks a question to be answered by each child in a learning log. She asks them to write down an evaluation of how effective they think they were in giving directions or asking clear and precise questions. She asks for some sharing.
>
> She then asks the pair to discuss how well they did as a team — in terms of the social skills for the day. The teams set

some future goals for themselves if needed, or they might celebrate their success in some way. After some more class sharing of what goals the teams may have set themselves Kym repeats the process, but this time she focuses on the academic goals of the activity.

More recently, other writers have described two more elements of cooperative learning.

Heterogeneity

Another principle of cooperative learning, we believe, is that we benefit from the diversity of talents and gifts in those around us. Students who work in heterogeneous groups have greater appreciation and acceptance of difference. (Sapon-Shevin 1991)

Reciprocity

When students recognise that when I give of my best and everyone else in the group does too, I receive a rich reward for my commitment. Reciprocity is a notion that recognises the value in working together. It answers the child's first question about group work — why should I get involved? Without a sense of reciprocity, team learning will not work. (Cooper 1990)

When introducing the notion of cooperative learning to his class, Andrew had his students complete a class activity where success depended on everyone playing their part fully. First of all he had some children deliberately sabotage the activity. They discussed the benefits of cooperation. Then they successfully completed the activity. He followed this up by getting the children to research sayings and proverbs that emphasised the benefits of cooperation. Groups mimed a proverb in action for the rest of the class to guess. They then made up their own list of benefits of cooperation and a team motto that reinforced this.

One team's motto read: All for one and one for all. When we cooperate, we have a ball.

Cooperative learning and inclusion

Some cooperative learning texts and support materials tend to follow a structural approach using clearly defined strategies (such as think-pair-share, round robin e.g Kagan 1990), while others see cooperative learning as much a part of a social process as much as it is learning. (Sapon-Shevin 1991; Dalton & Boyd 1992)

We believe that the latter is more appropriate in inclusive classroom. It is the notion of cooperative learning going beyond the usual learning situation into issues, relationships and living that are both influenced by and influence the student's everyday life experiences.

To develop a social/cultural perspective, we must first believe in the value of learning and living with others. Then we must lead students through a process that will:

- identify and teach basic group skills, e.g. turn-taking, using names, listening, participating (see Collis & Dalton 1989)

- promote the idea of power of one, e.g. shared resources, expertise, space, time, one goal, one role to perform, one product (Moorman 1993)

- build group maintenance skills, e.g. inviting participation, affirming, negotiating (for examples, see Hill & Hill 1990)

- build community, belonging and appreciation of diversity, e.g. games, activities, esteem builders (for examples, see Kagan 1990)

- develop skills of reflection, e.g. observation sheets, social and academic skill debriefing (for examples, see Bellanca, Fogarty & Dalton 1992)

- develop higher level thinking skills and group thinking processes, e.g. concept mapping, brainstorming, analysis, metacognition (for examples, see Wing Jan & Wilson 1993)

- challenge practices and values that exclude, e.g. simulations, debates, cooperative investigations (for examples, see Sapon-Shevin 1991)

We believe that cooperative learning is the most powerful means of developing an inclusive classroom to assist the full integration of special needs learners. It should not be confused with group work. Working in proximity to other students does not guarantee any of the above outcomes.

Peer tutoring: student-to-student

It's 1.30 and the children have come back into the classroom after lunch. Jane is a very capable reader who has been assigned as tutor to Hilary, a student who has moderate visual impairment and has a reading age approximately 3–4 years behind her peers.

To prepare for her role as a tutor, Mrs Lynch spent some time with Jane teaching her some word attack skills and some ideas for assisting with reading tutoring that she got from a teacher reference. She had Jane sit with her as she worked with Hilary while they did some reading with special texts that Hilary can read.

Jane spends 15 minutes per day working with Hilary. She displays patience and acceptance of Hilary's learning difficulties. Recently Jane wrote and illustrated her own story with pictures and collage for touching. It was written for Hilary on coloured cards and in large print. Hilary was absolutely thrilled at the gift. What made it special was that Jane wrote the story about the two of them bushwalking in a rainforest.

Mrs Lynch makes regular checks on Hilary's progress and just recently decided that she would trial some mathematics activities with Jane as the tutor. She has been impressed by the relationship that developed between the students. She has also noticed a gain in confidence on Hilary's part to attempt reading.

Teachers often utilise other students in a coaching or tutoring way, and we know that there are benefits to the tutor and the one being tutored (Topping 1988). But where we take time to prepare and help in the tutoring process there are many more outcomes possible.

Peer tutoring takes advantage of the notion of proximal development. That is, students of the same or near age sometimes have a deeper understanding of the learning processes of each other than does the teacher. It also allows all students to assume some caring, assisting role in the development of their less capable peers. It can be used with older and younger children and take advantage of the motivation in a different learning situation.

For the tutor there are new demands on them to think laterally, to praise and encourage, to review their own understandings, and their own self-esteem can benefit as well. The benefits include:

- enjoyment on the part of the student being tutored for the special attention and assistance from a peer or an older student

- the widening of friendships across the school

- one-to-one learning is less threatening and time focused than whole class instruction

- tutoring is expressed in the student's own language and context and this assists in the learning process

Teachers need to inform parents of the reason for and the benefits of a tutoring program. Many parents have seen tutoring as a form of cut-price teaching at their child's expense. Done well, communicated well, peer tutoring is a powerful teaching strategy with great benefits to all.

The following key points should be taken into account when setting up and using a peer tutoring program:

- select the task and process carefully — the tutor needs to understand what is required and how to go about it

- make interpersonal skills explicit — it may be necessary for the tutor to display more patience, rephrase questions or statements

- match the tutor and learner — use a sociogram perhaps as a means of finding suitable tutors

- give some basic training to tutors — of subject material, important processes, outcomes and so on

- make expectations clear — to both parties

- give tutors preparation time — they may need time to prepare materials, organise their thoughts

- provide good learning places — a special place for the tutor and student allows for better contact time

- get feedback from both — privately or as a pair ask them to reflect on the process, their understandings, their difficulties and how they handled them

- listen in frequently — monitoring is important

Mentoring: adult and student

Angela, the special education teacher, had just got back from a conference where she had heard great things about a mentor program at another school. She immediately discussed the possibility of this with her principal and the teachers at a staff meeting. There was strong support for the idea, provided suitable people and training could be found.

Angela worked with a local special needs consultant and a representative of the parent body to develop some criteria for selection and a list of ideal qualities or attributes. Advertising for mentors took place in the local community through church groups, retirement villages and parent groups. An information morning was held and 14 people attended.

Angela and the principal outlined the scheme and the way in which the volunteers would be used. Angela paid particular attention to the range of difficulties and needs that existed among the student group. The principal covered areas such as confidentiality, regular attendance and school support for the mentors-to-be.

The volunteers were asked to complete a sheet that asked for information about interests, hobbies, experiences and so on. They were asked to send the form back to the school after a couple of days to think about the commitment involved as a mentor.

A couple of weeks later, Angela met with a group of nine people of all ages and backgrounds and began their training. They covered a few areas such as assisting as a tutor, dealing with the unexpected, their role as a friend not as a teacher. She met each person individually and spoke briefly about the child assigned to the mentor. They met the teacher together and clarified visiting times and protocols.

A week later the mentor program began with a picnic at the nearby park where mentors and students met each other.

Mrs Crockett, who is 68, comes every week to visit her new friend Amy in year 3. Amy has spina bifida, is cheery and usually very positive. But Amy faces three operations in the next few months and will need support coping with her fears, and her absence from and return to school. Amy has no grandparents in the state and so Mrs Crockett has taken on a role akin to a surrogate grandmother. Amy loves the attention and the opportunity to be near a grandmother figure. They read together, practise spelling or do pre-writing activities. Amy shares her hobby of stamp collecting with Mrs Crockett. Mrs Crockett has taken to collecting stamps from her neighbours at the retirement home for Amy.

Mrs Crockett has played a very positive role in supporting Amy's return to the classroom after each operation. She made her a special doll to take to hospital and a cake for the class to celebrate her return to school.

In this book we describe mentoring as involving an adult in a role which may or may not be a teaching role. In the case of special needs learners, an adult sometimes represents confidence and competence in many life and learning skills. Adult volunteers can assist with basic routine things such as feeding, movement, drill and practice activities and simple exercises.

What frequently emerges in mentoring relationships is a deep friendship and trust between student and adult. There is an increase in confidence because someone can pay particular attention to the child's progress and development. That adult might share interests and take interest in the child's. In some cases, new perspectives on the learnings and difficulties of the child come to light.

Since a mentor is ideally a guide and 'big brother', 'big sister' or 'grandparent' figure, the person chosen must have certain qualities. Among the most important are patience, openness, confidentiality, love of children and a sense of joy. Mentors can be recruited through schools, church groups, aged or retirement homes, advocacy groups and relatives. They should receive some orientation on the nature of the child's condition and possible symptoms. They need to understand that they are not teachers but self-esteem builders. They must be aware of the need for confidentiality and respect. They must be suitable for dealing with and building a relationship with a special needs learner.

Look for mentors with a wide range of backgrounds. If the special learner shows an interest in art, then look for a potter or artist. If the child is musically inclined, then a mentor with a love of music or one who is an instrumentalist would be wonderful for them.

Mentors and students meet regularly — judged most appropriate by the teacher. Special needs learners can sometimes form deep attachments to their mentors and sometimes care needs to be exercised. Be sensitive to that attachment — do not change timetables and meeting times without warning. Make sure parents are informed and know the mentor as well — arrange a time for them to meet.

Above all, thank the mentor for the gift of themselves and watch as your circle of student support grows stronger and wider.

Curriculum adaptation

For many teachers, the most logical place to begin planning for an special needs learner is in terms of providing a curriculum that suits the needs and capabilities of that child. Using cooperative planning strategies and working with other teachers, librarians, aides, specialists, parents and so on, will greatly diminish the load and responsibility for developing curriculum programs that are innovative and child-need centred.

Teachers need to balance individual/specialist learning programs with interactive, cooperative ones. The following curriculum adaptations have been developed from the work of JoAnne Putnam (1991). As well as an individualised program with separate objectives, she identifies four levels of curriculum adaptation where the same learning objectives are addressed in different ways by:

- modifying the student response

- modifying the presentation of material

- reducing the workload

- lowering level/performance expectations

Modified student response

Nicole has limited sight and speech difficulties and has great difficulty in any reading/oral activity. She usually requires the assistance of others to be able to participate fully. Recently, the class was divided into groups of six to develop and then practise matching skills using flash cards.

The groups met and decided that the cards would work better for Nicole if they used quite large, brightly coloured fluoro-style cards on which they could put the information in very large print. They tested several cards and sizes of print until they found the right ones for Nicole. During the practice of the skill, Nicole was able to distinguish between the cards because of their size, and to help her, the children modified the game so that when they were pointed to by Nicole, they called out what was on their card. The children took responsibility for Nicole's learning, supporting her feeling of belonging, and their problem-solving skills aided her participation.

In some cases the response to the lesson might be given in a modified form.

- If the assignment requires oral presentations, then working in pairs will allow a child with a speech difficulty to help with the work and physical side of the presentation, while their partner speaks.

- Where a written response is required, a child with fine-motor or coordination difficulties might use a computer and printer, a picture board, a parent or peer who would scribe for them, or they might illustrate with concrete materials or models.

- Where the child is required to demonstrate mastery of a physical skill and they are limited to a wheelchair, the teacher might alter the requirements so that
  - a modified version could be played from the wheelchair
  - the child could develop a checklist of key skills to observe
  - the child could video classmates in action and help coach/critique their performance.

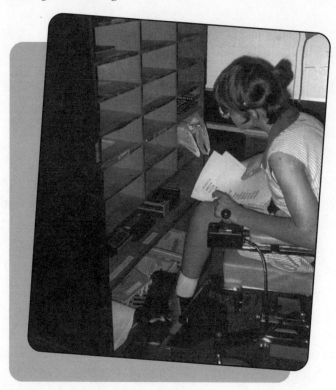

Modified presentation of material

Christian has been diagnosed as having Asperger's syndrome, a form of autism. He is demanding, narrowly focused and limited in his relationship and social skills. Teachers and students find that he has poor group skills, and tolerance and understanding of his limitations is needed. To make it more complicated, Christian is also very sensitive about being touched and working closely with groups.

In a recent mathematics lesson, where the class were introduced to number facts using group discussion, the teacher-librarian was able to suggest a computer program from a nearby resource centre that covered the same material. The program used colour, sound and animation to stimulate Christian's interest and participation.

The teacher was conscious of having Christian work with other children. So while the class covered the material in group sessions, Christian worked with the class support officer (who, in the U.S., would be a para professional). When he had mastered the material, he was asked to use his skills and knowledge to work one-on-one with another child. Because he had the skills and knowledge, he was able to feel more confident and not threatened by just the one peer. He repeated the exercise with several students. Not only was his knowledge deepened, but he had the opportunity to work with others where he felt more comfortable.

The objectives of the lesson are the same as those of the remainder of the class but the child receives the input, knowledge or instructions through another means.

- A child with a hearing impairment may need instructions to be written or on audiotape which can be played back at increased volume.

- A child with visual impairment might have another read to them or listen to taped material.

- A child with limited attention might have the material more fragmented and tied to smaller tasks in the same sequence. The teacher might employ additional colour, sound or movement in order to maximise concentration.

Reduced workload

Marla was born with Down's syndrome. She is loved by her classmates and participates readily in group activities, but is limited in the roles that she can take within her learning team.

She is able to practise certain procedural learning in her role as group resource supplier. She collects and distributes materials. In most group tasks the teacher allows the group to distribute or allocate work according to ability and level of difficulty. This happens in Marla's group when the teacher has not already assigned a specific task.

When the group works on the same task, the first person finished works in a tutoring or buddy system with Marla. Marla loves working with others and sometimes pesters the others for assistance. The teacher has a chart near Marla's desk that allows her to keep a record of tasks accomplished and mastered. Marla lets the teacher know when she has completed tasks and she places stickers on her learning chart. This has helped keep Marla on track. Her team members have also taken a very affirming interest in her chart and her progress.

Reducing the workload for a child might take a number of forms. The child will not accomplish the same amount of work in the same time as the other children so the teacher modifies the expected output or increases the time available. When the child's input or contribution to a group might be limited, group tasks might be shared to accommodate their special needs or skills.

Lower level expectations

Tyrone has fairly severe learning difficulties which include information processing and language delay, and the side effects of his medication for epilepsy adversely affect his concentration. The teacher has found that small short tasks work best and plenty of variety is required to keep Tyrone on task.

His teacher uses lots of collaborative learning strategies. Sometimes he works with his 'big buddy', Emily, from the upper school on reinforcement activities. Sometimes Emily develops games or puzzles on simple concepts or skills for Tyrone. He adores the attention and special relationship he has with his buddy.

At other times, the teacher uses the jigsaw strategy as a means of dividing up the group work to match needs and levels of ability. Like each child in the group, Tyrone works on his own special material which he brings back to the group. When he returns to his home team, Tyrone knows that his work is essential for the whole group's project to be completed. He feels valued and worthwhile by being able to contribute to the group's effort. The teacher benefits by being able to have one-to-one time with him during the activity.

There will be many times when the level of skills, knowledge or thinking process required will be beyond the capability or prior experiences of the special needs learner.

- A teacher might set lower developmental level tasks or may have the child work more frequently on skills closer to the beginning levels of Bloom's taxonomy, for example.

- A child with a significant information processing delay would find rote learning or mental style drills almost impossible to complete successfully. The use of concrete materials is better suited to reinforce such things as concepts, patterns and procedures.

- Another child with language difficulties, might have more sense of accomplishment and have written language experiences scaffolded for them by using a computer program. There are several that allow the child to choose from a range of plots, characters, language structures and formats. The modelling and the presentation possibilities would aid self-esteem and understanding. Educational resource centres and software dealers can provide excellent support in this area.

Individual education programs

Though known by a variety of names, the individual education program, or IEP, is a key structure to prepare adequately and professionally for a special needs learner. Essentially, the IEP is a means of coordinating what is known about the specific needs and conditions of the child with the available resources in a meaningful and relevant educational program. The provision of an appropriate IEP is dependent on:

- an understanding of the child's strengths and needs

- an understanding of the expectations of his/her parents

- clear and accurate information, on file or readily accessible

- suitable physical and personnel resources

- an action research approach that enables the teacher to continually reflect upon current practice and goals

When faced with the reality of having a child with special needs in their class, many teachers will immediately ask questions like these:

- What are his/her strengths and needs?

- How old is the student?

- What sort of behaviours does she/he exhibit?

- How do I plan for that child's needs?

- What kind of support or assistance will I get?

- Where did he/she go to school before here?

- Is there a student profile for me to look at?

Up-to-date information in clear and precise forms is crucial to understanding a particular child's circumstances. Teachers will look for information on physical, sensory or intellectual capabilities or perhaps on mobility, behaviour, social skills and therapy support. This information is important for the development of teacher skills, appropriate provision of resources and teaching strategies.

In most cases children with special learning needs will present to a school with a significant amount of information from medical and other sources. The purpose of an ensuing case review is to determine what specific support and needs the child has, in order for the school and teacher to make advance preparations if possible. In some circumstances though, this does not happen. A teacher will have little or no advance warning, consultation or involvement in the enrolment of a special needs student. And sometimes, important data is not recorded or asked for at enrolment time.

A basic goal of the inclusive classroom teacher is to educate the special needs learner within their classroom family as much as is possible. The IEP is a formalised process of dealing with very specific learning needs that cannot be addressed within the normal classroom context. It is built around the action research process and its focus is on a continuous cycle of planning, enacting, observation and reflection. This contrasts significantly with some other definitions of an IEP as being simply a plan of action to achieve goals specific to the child.

The individual education program is carefully planned and uses other resources and people as much as possible. It is focused on the current priorities of the child and is based on accumulated knowledge about the child.

The initial stage of developing an IEP is usually the result of a report, review, interview, assessment, observation or reflection. As far as practicable, it should be designed with the assistance of other care givers and professionals and will require ongoing focused evaluation or reflection to judge its effectiveness and impact on the child.

As a result of using an IEP, the teacher could hope to:

- prioritise and plan for specific needs

- provide a focused program specific to a child

- provide for a child's particular learning style

- develop closer and more professional links with all concerned for the child's education

- develop child-centred achievable goals and objectives

Your role in the IEP

The teacher is the professional whose expertise creates the learning episodes for the child. For special needs learners, there are other professionals and carers who also have a strong commitment to and investment in the child's future. Teachers need to be mindful of the often passionate feelings some adults have towards their special needs children. They have often struggled for recognition and support. They can be your best advocates and resource gatherers.

Who you gonna call?

When developing IEPs, teachers need to look beyond the usual professional associations and relationships. There are many who have a commitment or a capacity to participate in meaningful learning for a special needs child. Many parents, older people in the community, or people in advocacy positions have wonderful patience and offer friendly support when helping a child master the complexities of a task such as eating, holding a pen, manipulating materials or cutting up paper. Our use of these 'resources' is part of the way in which we build and maintain the inclusive classroom where all are valued. Figure 5.2 illustrates the range of support people that are available to most teachers of special needs learners.

Person	Relationship to child	Attributes
Parent	care giver prime educator	intimate knowledge of needs, commitment, love, concern, advocacy, support
Teacher	classroom/school carer learning steward	professional knowledge, observation and planning skills, developer of classroom climate, personal contact
Doctor	medical and other support	case history
Therapist	specialist support intervention, therapy	case history, special knowledge, specialist skills
Consultant	through teacher	special knowledge, pedagogy, resources, teacher networks coordinator
Advocate groups	through parents peer support	intimate knowledge of needs, resources, advocacy, parent support
Aide	classroom carer	personal relationship
Teachers	school community members teachers	expertise, peer support, other perspectives
Principal	school administrator	advocate, resource broker
Volunteers	caring adult	age, friendship, personal support
Students	peers	age, understanding, concern, cooperative learning

Figure 5.2 People power chart ▲

Ways to develop and use IEPs

There are five forms that we recommend for use in the development and review of IEPs:

1 Record of interviews

2 IEP: Major goals for term

3 Action research plan and reflection

4 Cumulative observation record

5 Student review summary

The use of these forms is at the discretion of the teacher, but the context for their use requires some explanation.

We see teachers as professionals, engaged in ongoing reflection and self-review. Reflection takes us into metacognitive awareness of our craft, our reasons for action and our decision-making processes. It allows us to draw upon our strengths through self-review. Research shows that where our reflection takes place in partnership with a peer, the potential outcomes are greater. (Garmston 1987)

Therefore, we see the need for teachers working with special needs students to continually critique and review their goals, their teaching and learning strategies and the outcomes. The five forms used provide a way of drawing upon all the concerns, information, talents and expertise of those people outlined in Figure 5.2.

Action research

When working on an individual education program, there can be long-term and short-term goals. Short-term goals might arise quite unexpectedly as a result of changing conditions, abilities and competencies. Longer term goals might need to be subdivided into achievable, observable short-term ones.

A goal such as becoming an independent eater might need to be considered against what skills are present now, what help is needed and what skills need to be developed to promote independence. The teacher might break these broad goals down into things such as unwrapping, holding spoons or placing food on a table. Sometimes, working with special needs children requires us to examine, in detail, much of what we take for granted. It can be humbling and challenging.

Figure 5.3 shows that the IEP is never complete. In a sense there is no beginning either. Because we constantly plan in the light of gathered information, observation and feedback, our reflective times allow us to then interpret the consequences, meanings or future actions that arise.

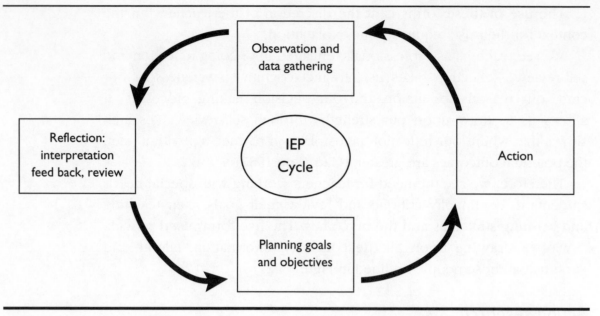

Figure 5.3 The cycle of IEP planning ▲

To make use of the IEP process, consider that:

- action does not take place without a knowledge of the needs of all parties

- information gathered must be a mix of focused and anecdotal observation

- reflection works best when it engages all parties in constructive feedback and interpretation

- planning to achieve goals and objectives becomes meaningful and relevant if it arises out of carefully focused review

Forms, processes and goals

The following descriptions of the use of the forms are part of gathering together information and data, providing feedback and review, and deciding on appropriate future action that matches the real needs of the child. Through this information we are trying to make the picture clearer; the action more precise and meaningful. We are maintaining records to achieve greater understanding of the child and their development.

1 The record of interviews

This form is a way of keeping track of all interviews in relation to a student. There is space to record the date, the participants, their relationship to the student, the issues that are discussed or arise and what action will be taken. Many teachers of special needs students begin the school year armed with information gathered from meetings with parents, therapists, consultants and so on. The record of interviews allows them to maintain a continuous record of issues and actions arising from such discussions.

These issues and actions can be summarised as part of the student review summary, to inform parents and others at reporting time.

2 The IEP major goals for the term

This form is a useful way of recording the goal, action and objectives for a student. The objectives are considered in terms of where the child is at now and in the future — the beginning point and the desirable end point. The personnel column records who will be involved in achieving the goals and, if possible, how they will contribute. Dates enable teachers to remind themselves of the need to review progress and processes. They also provide a developmental history of student achievement and how their needs were addressed.

The example of a completed goals sheet shows how major goals can be subdivided into measurable objectives and tasks.

3 Action research plan and reflection sheets

The action research plan sheet usually begins to be filled in when an issue or need arises. But it should also be considered as part of an ongoing process of self-review. It is best done in consultation with someone else, preferably a trusted peer — a person with whom the teacher has a professional and personal rapport.

The phases of developing an IEP action research plan are as follows:

a Identifying the need/issue:

- what is it?
- where did it come from?
- what have you done already?
- what success did you have?
- are there other students with similar needs?

b Addressing the need/issue:

- express this plan in teaching or action form
- describe what support you will need — be specific
- include as many people as possible
- attach actual strategies, lesson plans, etc.

c Peer support:

- what role/s will buddy assume? (observer, reflector, team-teacher, coach, resource, co-planner)
- describe how they will perform this role — be specific
- describe your role in the partnership

d Data collecting and review:

- what information will be recorded and how?
- who will do this?
- who will have access to the information?
- when will you get together for feedback and discussion?

e Summary of action plan

- include the why, how, who, when and where in short form

The reflection sheet is a vehicle for collecting the information and recording the feedback and interpretation after putting the above plan into action. The peer teacher for example might help the teacher to interpret observations that she made anecdotally during a science lesson. The peer teacher or teacher aide might observe the student in a very specific setting, looking for particular responses or outcomes.

Together they examine the information gathered. They look for links, consequences and implications. They discuss who may need to be aware of their discussions. They look at possible future action. A summary of their findings might be recorded elsewhere for future discussion with parents, therapists, consultants, etc.

The IEP cycle is the continuous process of targeting specific needs and issues and will always give rise to new understandings and future directions.

Record of interviews

School .... Sunnyvale Primary

Student .... Michael Anderson   Date of birth .... 18.10.87   Home contact .... Margaret & John Anderson

Telephone .... 736 2059   Year level 2   Class teacher .... S. Garsden

Date	Participants	Relationship to student	Issues	Action
12.3.94	N. Marshall S. Garsden	Speech therapist class teacher	• difficulties with social interaction in class	develop social skills program for whole class – work with speech therapist
17.4.94	M. Tarrant Margaret and John Anderson	behavioural psychologist parents	• what causes Michael's problems with social interactions	gather data through observing reactions to certain situations e.g. taking turns in games.
20.5.94	S. Garsden C. Burton M. Allenby	class teacher support teacher principal	• discuss Michael's problems with completing class work	ask for occupational therapy assessment

IEP Major Goals for Term

Student .... Sally Rowen

Date of birth 26.9.82

Class .... IV Blue

Teacher .... C. McIntyre

Goal	Action	Objectives		Personnel	Date Commenced	Date Reviewed
		Beginning point	Desirable end point			
To improve computer skills	Provide 3 x 30 minute sessions per week with teacher aide	Sally chooses to work within a limited range of desktop options	To explore a range of other maths programs during individual work time	Teacher aide, Mac computer. Selected programs - contact dealer and technology support centre	April 21	June 18
To increases independence in eating lunch at school	Arrange for Sally's class learning team to eat with her. Preparation required. Encourage Sally to unwrap lunch and eat faster.	Sally still asks for lunch to be unwrapped. Takes up to 40 mins to finish eating. Needs constant motivation to persist. Prefers adults to fuss over her.	To speak with class members about Sally's needs. Enlist their cooperation. Monitor eating time.	Class learning team and lunch time supervisor.	April	June
To increase Sally's reading skills – especially comprehension	Use sequenced comprehension skills program	Sally reads quite well orally - but CANNOT RETELL what she has read.	Sally should be making logical connnections in information read. Use cooperative learning team structures for mastery and understanding.	Class teacher Librarian – selected resources Learning team	May 4	June 8

78

IEP Action Research Plan

- Describe the issue or learning situation you want to investigate:
  Student unable to change from one learning situation to another without major upset and disruption to class

- What have you tried already?
  quiet time, teacher assistant to help, student helper

- What success did you have?
  minimal success with student helper, quiet time could work, but needs too long

- Are there other students who present with similar needs?
  3 other students tend to be extremely disruptive when activities are changing

- What action do you want to take?
  work out some cueing system to smooth out change overs

- What support will be required and from whom?

  Physical resources: video camera

  Specialist support: Integration support teacher
  Guidance/Behaviour management officer

  Teaching assistant:

  Parents/adults: Learning assistance tutor

  Students/peers: Class learning teams

- Role of action research buddy
  (possible roles: observer, reflector, team teacher, coach, resource, co-planner, etc.:
  I'd like guidance officer to observe what actually happens when changing lessons, and support teacher to share information of student's learning difficulties.

- What will be recorded and how?
  anecdotal, also actual words and actions - mine and the students - perhaps video

- Summary of plan (include why, who, how, when, where)
  Guidance officer - to record change overs on video.
  Support teacher - inform on learning needs.
  Tutor - practise (role-playing) how to get started.

4 Cumulative observation record

The cumulative observation record is a simple way of keeping track of student observations that are:

- **focused** (i.e. planned: looking at skills, attitudes, processes, knowledge and so on)

- **anecdotal** (i.e. unplanned, but considered significant or noteworthy)

This record is an ideal way of keeping track of the many incidents that need further investigation or clarification with parents, specialists, peers and even the student. Being both focused and anecdotal, they allow for a wide range of observations. They enable teachers to have more relevant information to report on when needed. Special needs learners very often require specific information about their achievement of milestones and key skills in a way that is rarely provided for in standard school report forms.

5 Student review summary

This is the final part of the formal recording of the IEP process. It may be used to accompany a school report, although teachers could feel more comfortable delivering its contents by way of an interview.

We recommend that a student review occur at least twice a year and include people such as the parents, consultant, principal, class teacher and others with a significant stake in the child's progress and development. The child might also be considered as a member of the interview/forum, at least in part.

The format allows for the recording of all relevant information about the student's growth, achievements and difficulties in the areas described. The others present are invited to discuss the outcomes or the implications of the information. It is critical that the interview includes some record of ongoing action. This might be in terms of a definite action, or as an affirmation — that is being done, is working well.

Above all, celebrate what has been done and what is happening. Look for the contributing factors to success. Build on those to help with the areas of greatest need.

Action Research Plan – Reflection Sheet

Decription of issue:
Concerned about the disruption caused each time teams/class change activities, too much time is being wasted - difficult to get everyone focused on tasks. Find myself getting trapped into negative responses which greatly affect the cooperative learning atmosphere in the class.

Information gathered:
Megan is extremely slow to change activities, she demonstrates confusion about the task expectations and where materials are to be found. She is easily side tracked and starts to play with other equipment she finds.

Feedback:
Video taken by guidance officer shows how other students are interacting with Megan. Issue is compounded by their comments and behaviour.

Interpretation of feedback and data:
Megan does have processing problems which make it hard for her to re-orientate herself with a different activity. If she has to move too far away from her task she becomes distracted and forgets what she has to do. Responds to taunts of others - takes this very seriously.

Implications for teacher, student, others:
Be super-organised with lesson plans, state/provide clear objectives for students.
Limit amount of verbal interaction needed for change-overs.
Be aware of level of participation Megan is capable of.

Possible action:
Provide written/visual objectives
Develop cue system for Megan e.g. we're going to change to different work in five minutes. Look at the clock. Start to get ready.
Work on team responsibility for behaviour

Date _____26.4.94_____   Signed _____J. Smiggins_____

Cumulative Observation Record

School .... Sunnyvale Primary

Student .... Megan Watson   Date of birth 12.4.85

Home contact .... Patricia Watson   Telephone 967 2317

Year level 5   Class teacher .... J. Smiggins

Focused Observation Records

Date	Specific skill / task	Observation/notes
27.4.94	Asked teacher aide to work through maths exercises with Megan	difficulty with concept of subtraction – handles addition reasonably well
28.4.94	Exercise program – health & fitness	Megan experiences problems keeping up with music - began calling out rudely to others
4.5.94	Spelling games	Megan seemed to become confused about when it was her turn
6.5.94	Comprehension activity	could not remember sequence of events in passage
8.5.94	Craft lesson	seemed to find fine motor tasks very unpleasant - avoidance strategies – wandering around classroom

Anecdotal Observation Records

Date	Specific skill/task	Observation/notes
28.4.94	group spelling activities	couldn't find pencil or work book – desk very untidy – went to class pencil jar, started sorting out all pencils needing sharpening
29.4.94	maths – measurement activity	responded to Paul's comment by using rude sign – constant disruption – no measuring done
3.5.94	shared reading time	argued with Mary about sitting on a particular chair
5.5.94	changing after swimming class	took 20 mins to get back to class – still no shoes and socks on. More time wasted

Student Review Summary

School .... Mountain View Primary ....

Student .... Sally Rowen .... Date of birth .... 26.9.82 ....

Home contact .... Helen & David Rowen .... Telephone .... 323 7615 ....

Year level .... 6 .... Class teacher .... C. McIntyre ....

Date of review .... 24.6.94 .... Period of review .... 6 months (semester) ....

Numeracy	Language/Communication
Seems to have little understanding of money even though basic addition skills are a relative strength.	Word recognition and spelling skills are improving. Has limited range of strategies to interpret texts. Usually needs help with any inferential tasks.
Ongoing action	**Ongoing action**
Involve Sally in a real-life money skills numeracy program e.g. class shop, cooperative games	Class teacher & support teacher co-plan a suitable comprehension skills program.

Motor (fine-gross)	Hearing, visual, other
Will soon be getting electric wheelchair from Spastic Centre. Uses index finger on left hand to operate computer	Hearing background noise/voices can be a problem. Visual difficulties slow Sally down with completion of tasks in class.
Ongoing action	**Ongoing action**
Support teacher will help by organising "learn-to-drive" mobility program and implementing this during sport times. Inform students of need to encourage Sally with keyboard skills.	Develop awareness with class of importance of work noise levels. Enlarge texts. Limit amount of information on one page.

Raising awareness: preparing for inclusion

What processes should a school have in place to ensure that inclusion can happen in a socially just way, and that allows teachers to feel sufficiently supported and confident to take on the extra challenges that inclusive teaching demands? Who needs to become aware?

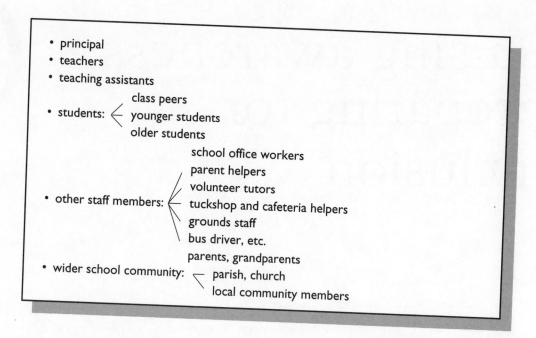

- principal
- teachers
- teaching assistants
- students: ← class peers / younger students / older students
- other staff members: ← school office workers / parent helpers / volunteer tutors / tuckshop and cafeteria helpers / grounds staff / bus driver, etc.
- wider school community: ← parents, grandparents / parish, church / local community members

Figure 6.1 Who needs to know? ▲

The whole school community is involved in the education of each and every child, some of whom have more special needs than others. For example, Christopher with cerebral palsy is in one teacher's class this year but this does not mean that every other teacher on the staff relinquishes responsibility to contribute to Christopher's education and social development.

Much of the resistance against inclusion is based on fear — fear of the unknown. If a teacher has no previous knowledge or contact with anyone who does not walk, talk, eat or play in what has come to be the accepted social way, then it is understandable that anxiety and apprehension will prevent immediate and unconditional acceptance. Preparation for inclusion should allow teachers a forum to express how they feel, but also encourage them to justify their stance. Values will be challenged and people will have very different reactions.

Awareness meetings

Exclusion of special needs students has often happened in the past because the extra demands were too onerous and the child was considered something of an inconvenience. Teachers can be concerned they will not receive enough support. Instead, a more positive approach of shared responsibility and team problem-solving to utilise available support and resources will facilitate and enhance inclusion.

It is necessary to develop a process for information sharing about new students. Discussion about students with special needs takes more time; it cannot be a quick chat in the corridor. We have used the process of awareness meetings effectively. Its purposes are to:

- raise awareness of inclusion itself

- reassure and inform the class teacher

- develop the notion of shared professional responsibility

- provide an appropriate structure which will result in a comprehensive profile of the child

- encourage personal reflection

This awareness meeting is a valuable information-sharing time. Through asking, answering, and discussing the points listed, stakeholders can develop a preliminary understanding of the child. This meeting would most likely happen before the student arrives at the school, either at the beginning of a new school year, or when a new student is enrolling. If the child arrives unannounced, the meeting should be held as soon as possible.

The following sample meeting shows the quality of discussion generated by this process:

Jordan will begin the first year of primary school after the summer holidays. The enrolment process has been completed and the integration support teacher has arranged to meet with the class teacher. The class teacher asks the questions provided, and answers are given, in this case, by the support teacher, who has been responsible for seeking out information about Jordan from his previous educational setting.

Support teacher. The basic background information on Jordan is that he is six years old and has attended a special education developmental unit (SEDU) for his pre-school year. The SEDU staff have been very helpful in providing a number of reports and other relevant information. As part of the enrolment process, I visited Jordan at pre-school, and at the end of last year, he came here with his parents for a visit. He seems a timid little fellow, preferring just to smile rather than answer when spoken to.

Class teacher: Can you give me a name or description of Jordan's problem?

Support teacher: Jordan has been diagnosed as having autism by the Autistic Association. He presents with many social, behavioural and communicative difficulties, which is typical of children with autism. Here are copies of notes from the Autistic Centre's education consultant. There is valuable information about autism and many of the characteristics Jordan displays in his social interactions. You might like to take some of these now, or all of them if you wish, and we can get together at another time to discuss what we have learned.

Class teacher: How did this condition come about?

Support teacher: Autism is a neurobiological disorder. It is probably influenced by biological factors. There is some evidence of genetic influences. Research into autism is continuing and there are still many aspects of the disorder that are uncertain.

Class teacher: What physical challenges does Jordan face?

Support teacher: Jordan can run and play but seems to lack the stamina of his peers. He is a poor eater and chooses to eat from a limited range of foods. He does not like fruit at all, and it is probably the texture or smell of many foods that he finds distasteful ... his parents struggle with this constantly. Jordan can also cause himself to vomit at will. Apparently he uses this strategy very effectively as a way of getting attention, particularly from his mother, or as a way out of what he perceives to be a stressful situation. His visual-motor planning is very poor and he finds holding a pencil firmly enough to write quite difficult. He also experiences considerable distress when asked to participate in games with others. He is very attached to his mother and finds leaving her at schooltime stressful.

Class teacher: What medical information do you have about Jordan?

Support teacher: Jordan is presently taking medication prescribed for attention deficit disorder. His 'at-home' behaviour is often quite disruptive and he is not a good sleeper. His mother is not sure the medication has improved anything at all, as Jordan has now begun waking during the night. She is considering stopping the medication. Jordan's behaviour at pre-school caused no unrest at all, so there is no need to expect behaviour difficulties here.

Class teacher: What are Jordan's strengths? What can we build on?

Support teacher: Jordan has good visual matching skills. He enjoys putting puzzles together. He is super-tidy! Always packing things up and putting them back where they should be. He responds well to photographs and is fascinated with landscape pictures. A possible way to begin reading would be to tap into these interests — adding print under the pictures, using his need for repetition and pattern. He seems able to learn routines quite readily, quickly establishing a ritualistic sequence to daily events. This could be an advantage when teaching him how to work in class. His play is parallel to that of his peers. He seems to be playing with other children but, if you observe him closely, you will see that it's almost as if there's an invisible wall between him and the others ... he never really joins in.

Class teacher: What can you tell me about Jordan's parents? Have they come to terms with Jordan's difficulties?

Support teacher: Jordan's parents are extremely supportive and interested in being actively involved in his education. They were relieved to know that our school was happy to enrol him. They have spoken about their earlier frustrations and are still adjusting to the fact that Jordan has a lifelong disability. They find his limited language use and rigorous adherence to routine disrupts the whole family. His younger sister is quite tolerant of his 'aloofness' and finds ways to coax him into playing and talking. I would suggest that the parents would appreciate strong support from us and the whole school community.

Class teacher: What extra support does Jordan need? Is there likely to be a therapist involved? Could therapy sessions happen effectively in the classroom?

Support teacher: Arrangements have been made for our systemic occupational and speech therapists to visit very soon to assess Jordan's needs. They have already been sent the most recent reports from the pre-school, so are aware we will need help to get started with suitable programs. Until then, I think we should be able to work out interim programs following the suggestions from the pre-school therapists. Are you happy with that? I have some sample activities here in this folder. The therapists prefer to work in the classroom, involving other children, but there may be times when it will be more effective to withdraw Jordan for specific skill sessions. By having the therapists work in the classroom, you are given an opportunity to observe what's done, and you are then able to back up the therapist's work.

Class teacher: Is there any specialised equipment or resources needed to work with Jordan? Where will I find these?

Support teacher: There is already an effective network set up to support Jordan. The Autistic Centre is on call, the therapists will visit regularly, and the various education libraries, especially the Low Incidence Support Centre, have a wide range of teaching materials and kits. These would be available for you to borrow ....

In this meeting structure, the class teacher asks the questions, takes note of the support teacher's responses and is actively seeking information about the student, which she needs to know to be prepared for inclusive planning and practice. At the end of the meeting the class teacher goes away with her own notes, as well as 'expert' information. The support teacher feels satisfied that she will be able to work well with this teacher, who seems open and willing to develop shared ownership of Jordan's education.

Of course, the support teacher had carefully prepared for this meeting by reading the files thoroughly and becoming familiar with the specialised information. It is important to note that descriptors used should be within reasonable understanding of the classroom teacher. Too much medical jargon can be quite threatening, especially to teachers who have had no close experience with physical or intellectual disabilities. Pressure can often be placed on support teachers to bring in the 'quick-fix kit', or wave the magic wand.

Anxious teachers can also present as angry or unhappy teachers, so awareness of the probable needs of the new student and the support structures available to them will relieve stress.

Throughout the awareness raising process, it is also important to allow the class teacher enough space to develop her own perceptions of the child. Each teacher has special gifts, skills and talents to bring to the educational arena. What a loss it would be if the experts were too prescriptive in their recommendations. Acceptance of the child as class member depends on the teacher feeling responsible and competent enough to deal with classroom situations involving the child. Teachers need to feel they can make decisions about how they want to teach to include children.

An extra dimension is added when outside 'experts' are invited to be part of the educative/caring team. Everyone has something to offer, even though some educators hold more definite opinions than others, and some feel more confident in their classroom practice than others.

In North America there are some procedural differences. Each child with special needs is seen by the school psychologist who consults with the child's physician.

The importance of recording

Keeping and maintaining appropriate records is good teaching practice. In the case of special needs learners, this is done for many reasons:

- establishing the exact nature of learning disabilities and what strategies need to be used in the educational process

- recording relevant information about support services and personnel

- recording developmental milestones

- recording significant events in the life of the child that might impact on school participation

- goal-setting, focused observation and anecdotal records

- recording of interviews with parents, carers, therapists, visiting teachers, etc.

- term and semester style reporting to parents

- keeping information about past learnings, conditions, issues, interventions and treatments that might impact on current learning

- planning for future action or review of programs undertaken

Anecdotal records

It is extremely effective to have a system of recording anecdotal observations of classroom behaviours and responses. This provides a focus for meetings and contributes to the ongoing building up of a comprehensive profile. This type of observation informs therapists, doctors, psychologists and other specialists. These professionals, members of the wider team working with the child, have no other way of developing 'the big picture'.

One child psychologist, after receiving a collection of a child's artwork with descriptions of the tasks and detailed notes of the child's intriguingly different responses, gratefully thanked staff for their efforts. He said how the case had been concerning him. Having access to the information compiled by teachers had shown him that there were definitely missing pieces to the puzzle that he had not previously considered. This child, although able to read and write seemingly efficiently, has extreme difficulty comprehending the subtleties of meaning within texts. A word can trigger off random thought patterns which take him far from the learning task at hand. He finds concentration difficult, and usually presents with a stressed, wide-eyed gaze in class.

Making detailed notes of the day's happenings is not always practical for the busy class teacher, so the educative team could work out the way they feel most comfortable with, to record anecdotes as they happen, or soon after. This example of such a record sheet is offered as one way to tackle the task.

Observation Notes

Child's name **Matthias Schmidt**   Teacher **G. Royland**

Date	Activity/lesson	Observations
20.4.94	Whole class maths lesson – addition – working from blackboard.	Matthias appeared to be very distant and seemed unable to concentrate on the 'teaching talk'
3.5.94	Group activities with language skills	M did not contribute well – rubs eyes and frequently blinks
9.5.94	Science experiments – measuring with water and other liquids	M seems to have difficulty judging when to stop pouring liquid. Looks surprised when he spills some by pouring too much.

Implications

Perhaps M's eyes are causing him difficulties. Ask team about next step. This could solve a lot of problems!

Specific student profiles

Relevant information and data on a student's case history and special needs can inform teachers and carers about the type of learning support the child needs. The student information profile (SIP) is designed to gather significant information about the child in terms of:

- the nature of the special needs

- the exact impact of these needs on school/social functioning

- a summary of any assessment — linguistic, numeracy, psychological, social, medical, therapeutic, etc.

- a list of current support service being utilised

- previous education history (if any)

It is possible for other relevant people to complete some aspects of the profile. Parents, doctors, therapists, previous teachers and special needs support teachers can all add to the compilation process.

Completing an SIP

Part A contains information about the nature of the student's disability. The description might contain specific names for conditions such as Asperger's syndrome, spina bifida, mild epilepsy or cortical visual impairment. Teachers could then review relevant literature or contact support networks for sufferers, to gather more specific information on the condition and its impact on a child's life.

Part B gathers information about the child's level of mastery or relative competency in a wide range of areas. Indicating a level allows the teacher and those working closely with the child to have a simple yet accurate picture of the child's capabilities within the school setting. This can help with simple reminders such as placing the child in the best seating position if they suffer from hearing or visual loss, or in the choice of concrete mathematics materials where hand functioning is limited.

Part C is a section where specific results from assessments can be maintained. Teachers need to be mindful of the confidentiality of some of this information and may need to discuss with their principals any plans to share this information.

Student Information Profile: Part A

School ...... Mountain View Primary

Student ...... Sally Rowen   Date of birth 26.9.82

Home contact ...... Helen & David Rowen   Telephone 323 7615

Year level 6   Class teacher ...... C. McIntyre

Nature of disability	Description
Physical	Cerebral Palsy (oculometer abraxial) Mild epilepsy Cortical Visual Impairments
Intellectual	• moderate to severe impairments • difficult to test as Sally must use keyboard to write answers
Sensory	• indicates poor integration of body movements — easily startled - tends to panic when driving wheelchair herself
Language	• expressive and receptive • processing difficulties
Social	• has difficulty maintaining conversations with age-peers • prefers to play with younger students
Emotional	• becomes easily stressed if class demands are too high • self-esteem fluctuates
Other	• needs a great deal of help and reassurance to begin new tasks.

Student Information Profile: Part B

Please record an appropriate level of mastery or competence.

Area		Level
Personal	Feeding	☐ Independent ☑ Minimal assistance required ☐ Moderate level of help: needs to be fed, helped with clothes, wiping ☐ Significant help needed ☐ Totally dependent: specialised help may need two people
	Toileting	☐ Independent ☐ Minimal assistance required ☐ Moderate level of help needs to be fed, helped with clothes, wiping ☑ Significant help needed ☐ Totally dependent: specialised help may need two people
Physical	Speech and Communication	☐ Normal or appropriate range ☑ Some loss: minor adjustments needed ☐ Moderate loss: may need aids or assistance ☐ Severe loss: help from aids, very limited
	Mobility	☐ Normal or appropriate range ☐ Some loss: minor adjustments needed ☐ Moderate loss: may need aids or assistance ☑ Severe loss: help from aids, very limited
	Hand functioning	☐ Normal or appropriate range ☐ Some loss: minor adjustments needed ☐ Moderate loss: may need aids or assistance ☑ Severe loss: help from aids, very limited
	Hearing	☑ Normal or appropriate range ☐ Some loss: minor adjustments needed ☐ Moderate loss: may need aids or assistance ☐ Severe loss: help from aids, very limited
	Sight	☐ Normal or appropriate range ☐ Some loss: minor adjustments needed ☐ Moderate loss: may need aids or assistance ☑ Severe loss, help from aids, very limited
Intellectual	Intellectual ability	☐ Normal or age appropriate range ☐ One year behind peers ☐ Moderate differences: 2–3 years behind peers ☑ Severe differences: 4–5 years behind peers ☐ Profound differences: more than 5 years behind peers
	Achievement	☐ Normal or age appropriate range ☐ One year behind peers ☐ Moderate differences: 2–3 years behind peers ☑ Severe differences: 4–5 years behind peers ☐ Profound differences: more than 5 years behind peers
Social/emotional	Behaviour	☐ Normal or age appropriate ☑ Some inappropriate behaviour ☐ Frequent misbehaviour, social problems ☐ Difficult: requires frequent intervention ☐ Dangerous to self and/or others
	Social relationships	☐ Normal or age appropriate ☑ Some inappropriate behaviour ☐ Frequent misbehaviour, social problems ☐ Difficult: requires frequent intervention ☐ Dangerous to self and/or others

Summary of Assessment: Part C

Language

Date	Test	Results	Comments
11.10.91 (C.A: 10.02)	Holborn Read. Age	7.03 R.A.	(previous teacher's assessment)
19.10.94 (C.A: 13.2)	Neale - Reading Ability	7.10 R.A.	related to intell. impairments

Mathematics

Date	Test	Results	Comments
22.9.94	Diagnostic Analysis	low scores in several areas	class program should involve basic rote-learning tasks

Psychological, social, therapy, other (If applicable)

Date	Test	Results	Comments
25.8.93	Speech Therapist Report	scaled scores range 1-6	needs extension in functional language areas
12.9.94	Intelligence Scale for Children		needs supportive school environment

Support services currently utilised: Part D

Nature	Contact person	Details
Speech and language therapy	N. Wrightson	Education Support Centre
Occupational therapy	A. O'Brady }	
Physiotherapy		
Guidance or counselling	V. Dunsford	District Edn Officer
Remedial/early intervention		
Visiting teacher:　　hearing		
(vision)	D. Strong	North Region Support Centre
(physical)	V. Ginley	
other		
Medical support		
Other		

Previous educational history: Part E

Newtown Special School until year 4 level.

....

....

....

Date　14.3.95　　　　　　　Signed　　C. McIntyre

Standardised assessments and the like do form part of the overall picture and will give some measure of progress. We strongly encourage teachers to remember that standardised testing is one way of viewing the child. It is by no means the only one. In some cases, an over-reliance on an IQ score or similar test severely impedes what we can do for a child. There is a real danger in teaching to the expectations of the test or creating self-fulfilling prophecies about the child. At all times look beyond the surface level.

Part D outlines any ongoing therapy that the child might be engaged in. By recording the therapist's name and organisation, we build up our own and the child's support network. Many teachers of special needs children will also take the opportunity to visit the therapist or have them visit the classroom. Some teachers watch or assist at therapy sessions to understand and gain a greater appreciation of the child's daily life and needs. There are some cases where teachers or their support officers must also be able to provide some therapies or physical assistance — providing substantial motivation for learning from other professionals.

Part E contains information about prior schooling or educational programs. To complete the jigsaw, many teachers will make contact with the child's previous educators to build up a more complete picture of the child.

Sharing information

What do the children need to know?

It seems to be a good idea to begin any awareness raising program at school level by encouraging the students to ask the questions. Perhaps small groups could work out a list of questions that have been bothering them. These can be collated on large sheets of paper, and arrangements made for these questions to be answered appropriately. Some questions can be answered on the spot; others may need to be researched, either by the teachers, or by groups of students. Asking the children what they need to know includes them and shares the responsibility for understanding the special needs. The teacher is inviting students to be part of the joyous process of teaching and learning inclusively.

Sometimes it becomes necessary to teach about certain conditions or differences. For example, it was necessary at one school to explain the reasons for a child having a shunt inserted to drain a cyst in her head. There were safety issues involved for the playground. Teachers were having difficulty convincing children that the child could be hurt. The support teacher suggested that the children might be more likely to respond positively to requests for appropriate behaviour if they understood the reasons why, so lessons were planned to inform the children about the basic workings of the brain. A diagrammatic model of the brain was constructed and explanations given about the position of the shunt and where the plastic tubing went all the way down to the stomach. The students who had helped construct the model were able to explain clearly why it was not wise to play too roughly with this child because if the tubing was blocked medical problems could occur. Hearing the same warning from peers seemed to make much more sense than hearing it from teachers.

Some months later, the class was able to revise the physiology of the brain, within the context of a language unit based on a study of the human body. Teachers planned together, and the integration support teacher worked with the whole class on a series of activities focusing on malfunction. The students were able to build on their previous knowledge of brain function, and were developing an understanding of the learning difficulties occurring when the connections between brain and body don't work properly. This was also an effective way for teachers to teach themselves about why some children have more trouble learning than others. It was then possible to say openly to the class such things as:

> 'David's brain doesn't seem to like learning to read. He will need some extra help from us.'
> 'Jessica's brain is not sending the right messages to her arms to let her catch the ball. Call her name and make sure her arms are ready before you throw.'
> 'My brain is not thinking clearly today. Could you read that to me again, please. I'll listen carefully this time.'

Parent and community awareness

At times, parents have been involved in these lessons and have then been able to inform the wider school community. Parent–teacher meetings, information nights and school assemblies are excellent opportunities for spreading the word about why and how. Many people are asking for involvement. Teachers have a certain responsibility to provide occasions when members of the wider school community can become part of 'the team'.

Parents of special needs students in Australia have said that they really don't have all the options available to other parents. Once they have managed to find a school willing to enrol their child, they have to stay around to deal with all difficulties that come along. They can't take the risk of moving schools, even if it would be more convenient for the rest of the family for example, if the school was closer to home. Many parents have to travel quite a distance to a school they feel is going to provide quality educational opportunities for their children. This is not the case in the United States where special needs students attend their local school.

The general parent population could learn more about the inclusive processes developing in the school. They need to know more about the learning difficulties the special learners have and what programs are being developed to assist them to learn effectively. If they are interested in knowing more about specific syndromes and conditions, the school should be prepared to offer opportunities for such information to be shared, such as social evenings and information sessions.

The gradual and consistent raising of awareness to get to a stage of whole school community awareness can take a long time, even years. When the ownership and shared responsibility of providing for all learning needs is coming from the wider school community, it is more likely to be lasting and self-generating. Parents of special learners will feel so much more comfortable knowing that everyone knows why their child looks, sounds, moves or learns differently. Conversations can be more relaxed and natural, with everyone knowing the answers to the awkward questions.

How enriching the whole inclusive process becomes! Teachers, parents and students all become far more knowledgeable about how bodies and brains work, and are then able to be more patient, more tolerant, more understanding of others' needs, less irritable if things don't work out smoothly, less patronising — in essence, more inclusive.

Sharing the records

With many special needs learners there must be time allowed for sharing information and results from a range of medical and therapy reports. This information can be shared at regular meetings. However, with some children who have multiple disabilities, the teachers and parents need to be talking almost daily about the effects of new drugs, if the child is generally feeling well, or how much breakfast was eaten, or what sort of behaviour is likely to be expected. There should be provision made for quick informal chats, usually at the beginning of the school day, and for regular, more formal reviews, perhaps each term.

What takes 15 minutes?

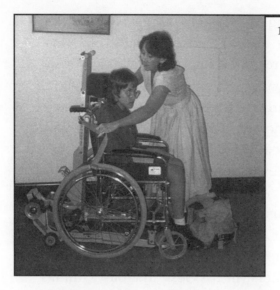

1 Time to go
   downstairs ...

2 Get strapped in

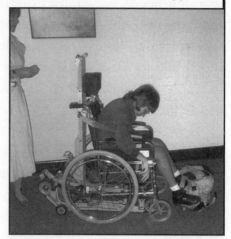

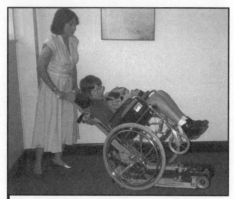

3 Brakes ... check
   Seat belt ... check
   Arms tucked in ... check
   Hold the school bag ... CHECK!

4 Tip me up and down we go!

5 Sing a song
   along the
   way ...

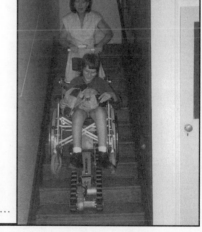

6 Second
   verse ...
   same as
   the first ...

8 Changing chairs …

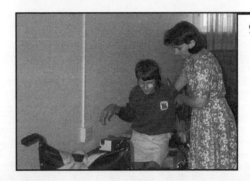

9 Turn and sit …

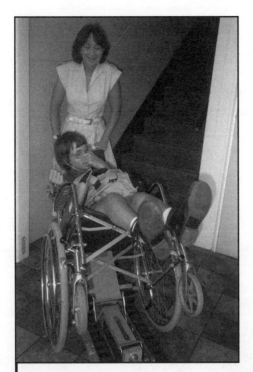

7 Oh! oh! hold the nose past the rubbish bins …

11 Off on my own … oh! what a feeling!

10 Getting strapped in again

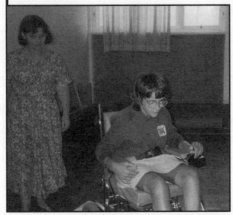

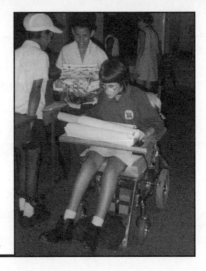

12 Helping out with changing classrooms.

7 Supporting inclusive practice

Many times we hear the cry from teachers that there is not enough support. Not enough help from the 'experts' to make inclusion work. We understand how difficult it is for teachers to make the changes in their own thinking and teaching practice that are necessary for all children to have access to equal opportunity for quality educational experiences. However hard this shift may be, inclusion cannot become real and true without it. So, we keep on asking the hard questions. We keep on challenging teachers with examples of inclusive practice, so that the barriers will eventually crumble away, leaving a wider space for clearer vision. The hard questions must be asked, of all of us. The world is just full to the brim with different people. There's no getting away from differences. So, accepting that differences are an integral part of life is the first step.

We can all make choices! We can make the choice to embrace the differences in our students and develop inclusive classes. Sadly, many teachers choose to categorise and segregate special children, and in doing so, increase their own workload. There are support structures within schools, in the wider educational arena and the community. There are so many organisations and agencies in fact, that it would not be feasible to list them here. Instead, we would prefer to provide a few ideas about where help can be obtained. Also, an example of the support network built up for one particular child will be shown.

Personal support systems

Teachers need to develop their own personal and professional support systems. As we mentioned earlier, working in the area of inclusion is heavy on emotional involvement. Emotive reactions and, in many cases, over-reactions get in the way of inclusivity. We see so many struggles going on, so many times when class teachers are struggling to come to some understanding of how they feel about having children with extreme special needs for learning, in their classes. We would suggest that many problems with inclusion come about because teachers have difficulty in accepting the very basis of inclusion — the acceptance of difference.

There is nothing to be gained from trying to 'normalise' a child with severe impairments. All children, however great or small their differences, can be respected and valued. The frustrations teachers can experience are sometimes not caused by lack of support. They may come about because there is difficulty in accepting difference.

What is support?

Many teachers believe support to be a physical presence: either a teacher or teaching assistant, a volunteer helper perhaps, who comes to the classroom to work specifically with the difficult child or children. Others prefer to receive support in the form of planning time, or discussions with the team of stakeholders.

It seems that when teachers really begin to take responsibility for the 'special' child, problems of 'ownership' arise. Who starts to make the decisions about curriculum? Who takes charge of the social skills training? Can we expect children whose personal relationships have always presented poorly to be able to relate to more than one teacher? The child can become confused and exhibit all those dreadfully embarrassing behaviours such as shouting out 'I hate you! You're not my teacher!' or stomping off to sulk in the corner for a while when not understanding what is expected. If the student becomes irrationally violent, either physically or verbally, then the situation is of course more difficult to negotiate, and there will need to be some plans of action in hand, in case of such emergencies.

These cases are quite extreme, and would be far from common. Diversionary tactics are often the best. There is no gain in a teacher confronting a confused and non-compliant student, demanding that the unwanted behaviour cease immediately. It is most often better to divert, wait a little while, and calmly model the appropriate responses. In preparing for such possibilities, teachers can provide immeasurable support for themselves, by investing in courses or workshops which are specifically aimed at developing quality negotiation and communication skills. Then it happens! Teachers, instead of feeling angry and frustrated, begin to reflectively distance themselves from the conflict, enough to understand the possibility of win/win, rather than win/lose, or at worst, lose/lose situations. Assuredly, the confused and frustrated child is not particularly enjoying feeling so angry!

Teachers — teach yourselves

But I don't know anything about Asperger's syndrome, or autism or receptive language disorders … Who is going to help me? How can I teach this child?

Take a deep breath! Adopt a proactive stance! Go and find out for yourself! The children need you to want to teach them well enough to find out information about their learning needs as they arise. You don't have to suddenly become an expert; just take little steps. Perhaps you could aim for one lesson, one session, or one day a week where you feel comfortable that your special learners are being catered for with materials and equipment, and that you have planned with inclusive principles in mind.

There are many agencies available to provide help for educators. The low incidence nature of most physical and intellectual impairments makes generalisations about what would be the best way to tackle a particular problem in the classroom rather impossible to make. There are growing numbers of autistic children enrolling in schools and there is quality information available from autistic associations or centres around the country. However, each child presents with a personalised set of characteristics, and must be dealt with accordingly. What works for one child may be quite inappropriate for another. Trial and error can be the name of the game, but the informed teacher is more likely to plan for successful inclusive learning than the teacher who chooses not to become informed.

Schools can build up files of information about the learning differences and needs of their own clientele, so that the same research never needs to be done twice. Updating is important though, and this should be done reasonably regularly.

Seminars are offered by a wide range of organisations to inform about specific disabilities or conditions, for example epilepsy, asthma, cerebral palsy, diabetes.

Children often present with a number of associated difficulties, so it is often necessary to understand the total impact on classroom learning.

Whether or not teachers master inclusive practice depends on what they really want for their students. Do they want their students to feel included? If so, then it can and will happen …

Be patient with the children, with yourselves and with each other.

The real world …

In reality, we will probably never be satisfied with the amount of support we are given, so we need to create our own. Take this situation as an example:

Erin has quite high support needs. The support network that has been built up around those needs is shown in figure 7.1.

When one need is satisfied or, most usually, brought to a manageable level, then the 'team' begins to work on the next one. Erin's difficulties, both physical and educational, are not fixable. She is learning to live with them, and so is the team. No one says it's an easy process … but it's challenging and rewarding, and as educators, very humbling. We don't have all the answers, and maybe we never will, but we're probably not expected to.

Erin loves being in school. She has good friends, her own age, who keep coming back to check if she has finished eating yet, so she can play with them. Sometimes she doesn't join in appropriately in class, and does what the kids call 'stiff donkey'. Maybe, just maybe, if our voices did not work, and we had to make such an extreme effort to try to communicate and be part of a group discussion, then we would demonstrate our frustrations by lying on the floor too!

Erin's needs and support network are discussed in some detail here, to illustrate how much support is actually available, if a team approach is used. There would not be huge numbers of children with such complex needs, so this extreme example is given to show how much can be achieved, when and if the need arises.

Because Erin cannot talk, she uses a voice output communication device called a Megawolf, which is about the size of a laptop. It needs to be programmed using a phonemic system, and overlays must be made using a computer

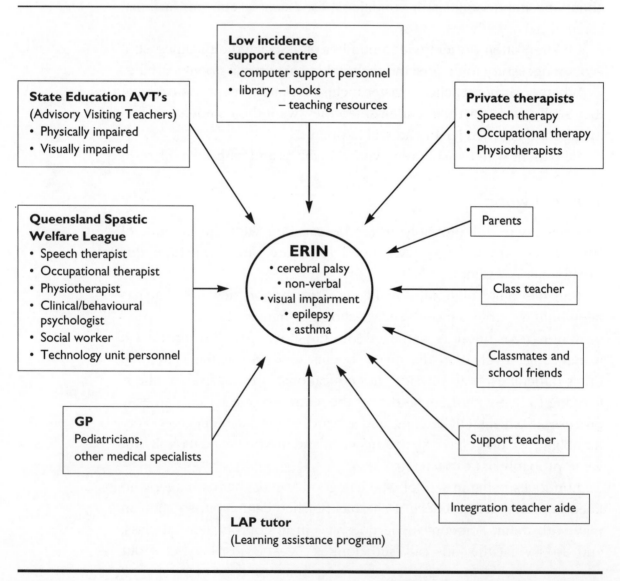

Figure 7.1 Erin's support ntework ▲

picture/word system, known as *compics*. Learning to program the Megawolf took some time, and we were anxious that we were disadvantaging Erin by not making fast enough progress mastering the process. The training meetings provided were after school and it wasn't always possible to get across town on time. We struggled along, congratulating each other when some small advance was made, but mostly feeling extremely technologically inadequate. It should be remembered that Erin was one of many special needs children in the school so support teacher time had to be shared.

Erin's class teacher was able to take on more responsibility for programming and had her own ideas about how she wanted to use the Megawolf to include Erin in class activities. Erin was able to answer as well as ask questions, because the teacher had carefully structured the lessons to allow for particular questions and answers. Sharing the load even further was possible with the speech therapist who began to prepare overlays through her technology support department.

All this time, Erin's mother was quietly working away building on her skills and experimenting with programming. Also, occupational therapy exercises have been concentrated on Erin's left hand, and she is now able to isolate her index finger to point and press the overlays more accurately. Erin's learning behaviour became much more compliant, motivation increased and her intrinsic desire to be praised for work well done led to more use of the Megawolf in classroom lessons. It is not a novelty any longer. We are at the stage now of planning ahead with the classroom teacher so that overlays with appropriate vocabulary are ready to enable Erin to respond in class as she would be able to if she could speak. This also makes it fun for other students to have a turn asking Erin questions, using the Megawolf themselves, and using a combination of signs and spoken language.

The support teacher will often present new material to Erin's classmates, and ask them to contribute ideas about how we can teach this to Erin. They understand how Erin's technology can help her, and they enjoy making up games to help her learn.

Peer helpers

Let us now take a look at another level of support. Each classroom is full of clever, efficient helpers ... your students. It's a good feeling to know that you have been able to help someone, and most children we have worked with over many years of classroom experience are only too happy to be included in the infrastructure of the inclusive classroom. They usually like to help, so cooperative learning holds many answers. The team-building strategies embrace the special learner, along with everyone else. There are many resources available to help teachers implement cooperative teaching and learning strategies. The philosophy of cooperative learning is inclusive, and brings a pervasive atmosphere of positivity and enjoyment to the classroom. Children who are learning to be valued members of a class are willing to value others.

Inclusive practice

Those classes where teachers are skilled in cooperative teaching and learning practice are the classes which welcome different children, without fuss and bother. These classrooms are **inclusive** through:

- teachers' skill and expertise in the craft of teaching

- flexible classroom management

- respect for other persons being modelled by the teachers

- a wide range of teaching and learning opportunities

Monitoring progress

To monitor the progress of children with extreme needs, an individual education program (IEP) should be prepared. Stakeholders are the class teachers, support teachers, therapists and parents. It seems too often to be a great temptation to emphasise the 'specialness' of the student, which tends to lead to an exclusive program, through its very individuality. We understand that there will be times when it is necessary and more effective to withdraw the student from the classroom for individual instruction, for example speech therapy. However, we believe that there are many types of 'special' lessons which could and should be happening in the general classroom situation. These lessons are often very interesting because of the 'special' resources used, so all students can benefit in some way from being given the opportunity to see, hear and use these resources.

Team effort

Inclusive practice allows for the spectrum of learning experiences and opportunities. As an educative team, sit together and plan for various groupings, types of lesson structures, situations, both inside and outside the classroom, which embrace differences. Always expecting a reading or writing product from a lesson can be exclusive practice. Many children have difficulty producing a quality written product, just as many children experience stress when expected to read aloud. What better way to develop an inclusive program than to invite as many stakeholders as possible to plan as rich a program as the ideas of many people can produce! Recent writings on IEPs all mention that the process is time-consuming and that most teachers find this yet another burdensome demand on their already overloaded time schedules. Yet, it is a task that must be done well if we are to be held accountable for the quality education of the children with special needs in our schools.

From experience, we understand that programming alone can be hard work. That is why we encourage cooperative planning. Start small — perhaps with just the social skills program, speech therapy, or occupational therapy, or one aspect of a more complex area, for example number or measurement in mathematics. Often, just changing the type of product, from a written summary, for example, to a group presentation, will provide the opportunity for any child with any or many impairments to be included.

Stakeholders should work together to see how the inclusive classroom will readily accommodate many areas of the 'special curriculum', thus reducing the need for an entirely separate or special program for each special child. Therapists are often quite willing to work with groups or whole classes, to explain or demonstrate the type of work they are doing with special needs children. For example, Erin's physiotherapist brought a model skeleton to her year 3 class to explain why Erin had to learn some new stretching exercises for the muscles in her legs. The children and teachers learned about high and low muscle tone. Her speech therapist always includes other students in activities when introducing new resources, ideas or technology. We often hear children talking to Erin in exactly the same tone, and using the very same phrasing that we have modelled to them.

Parents are special too

Most parents would agree that being a parent is rarely easy. Being the parent of a child whose needs are so extreme that a great deal of extra educational help is needed, or even of a child who finds it difficult to learn within an inflexible system which does not cater for different learning styles, is a frustrating and difficult idea with which to come to terms. The education system as a whole is not quite ready for the challenges presently arising, as special schools and a number of different types of institutions close.

Deciding on a suitable school setting and applying for enrolment should be quite a straightforward process. As a parent, one considers location, transport, educational reputation and standards. It is also important that the child enrolling will feel happy and comfortable and will make friends.

Parents and carers of children presenting with different physical, intellectual, emotional, cultural or socio-economic needs tell stories of feeling extremely excluded when asking that a place be provided for their child in the local community school. The process can turn into a gruelling experience and the friendly encouragement of a supportive school staff can be but a dream if schools are not prepared. Greatest difficulties seem to be experienced by the parents of children with physical or intellectual impairments. The school response is, of course, dependent on where that particular school community is on its journey of acceptance of difference.

If the need to consider what their school can offer has never been challenged by a child who needs more scaffolding than others, then staff will be faced with a need to consciously consider where they are in their own development as teachers and as members of a community. This is emotive territory. This is delving deeper than beliefs. This is getting right down to it and confronting values face to face. At a personal level, this sort of self-evaluative reflection can be uncomfortable.

Another point of view

Let's take a look at this situation from the parents' point of view. If a child's difficulties have been noticed early, even before the child is old enough for school, there will most likely have been a barrage of diagnostic tests. Parents will have stoically trooped from family doctor to pediatrician or physician, to clinical psychologist, behavioural psychologist (because all this one-to-one therapy often results in the

child developing quite a repertoire of manipulative behaviour strategies), to hospital-based therapists and so on, and so on … and on. The last thing a parent needs is to feel that the school, teacher and class are not all that willing to become involved in the education of their child.

As educators it is so very important to develop an understanding of the family and how family members are coping with the challenges of living with a special child. Teachers need to skill themselves up in the area of interpersonal communications, not only to simply cope with the many and varied situations that arise daily, but to be able to encourage and support parents and to promote growth.

What parents expect

To be sure that we were not making assumptions about the expectations parents have of teachers, we met with the parents of eleven students at a particular inner-city school which is quite a way along the inclusion journey. For some time now these parents have been encouraged to speak out about their feeling and fears, to identify and express their needs for support and to become involved in the awareness raising activities which are vital if true community acceptance and support are to develop. We have included some of these comments and opinions to show the parents' perspectives on quality inclusive education.

Saira has intellectual impairment, expressive language disorder (at times echolalic speech) and some inappropriate compulsive/obsessive behaviours. Carol is Saira's foster mother:

'The reaction of other parents to myself and Saira was very evident and quite negative when Saira first came to school here for year 1. We had already been through quite a process of trying to find a suitable educational setting for Saira so were probably oversensitive to the looks and remarks of others. So much depends on the teachers. If the teachers at the school have an acceptance of the child and demonstrate that acceptance to all students and parents, without reservation, then it is accepted that the special needs child has as much right as anyone else to be in the classroom. Class teachers need to understand that they have so much to offer the special needs child. They have something to give that specially trained people or therapists don't have.'

Erin's mother, Diane, told us:

'When Erin began school here in two years ago, children and parents stopped and stared. Now no one does! Erin is accepted and loved and she knows it. There's often a cry of 'We're not trained, we don't know how to deal with this' from teachers. As a parent of a child with so many difficulties it's hard to hear those sort of comments. Perhaps a good yardstick for teachers would be to always remember as teacher how you would feel if this child was your own. There's an extensive support network built up around the students here. It's a matter of being persistent and being able to identify what the needs are. Then together, parents and teachers can track down someone within the system who can help.'

Judy is Carmel's mother. Carmel is a ten-year-old student with Down's syndrome. She has speech difficulties and some intellectual delay. Judy said:

'Parents need to be patient, with the school and with the teachers. Sometimes this is hard because parents have some quite complex issues to deal with when their child has special needs of one sort or another. Many children are travelling quite a distance to attend a school that has been willing to accept them. This causes time hassles and can be extremely inconvenient for other family members. Legislation has now made it more difficult for schools to say 'no'. Children with special needs should be accepted into local schools, either government or independent. In the long run there would be less cost to the system. A change of attitude would have us thinking that to gladly take on the challenge offered to a school community by special needs children is indeed a great advantage for everyone concerned.'

Many parents at that meeting spoke of never really feeling welcome. Can this be that because their children are different they are expecting negative attitudes and responses from others? Perhaps this could be because they have not yet fully accepted the difficulties themselves, so assume that others will not be able to do so either. There is a cycle of grieving that can never end for families. There is a strong sense of grief and loss, knowing that this child is ours, we'll have to care for this child all our lives and no, we don't want your sympathy.

The feeling of not fitting in to the school community could, however, be due to a type of negligence. As a school staff we would need to consider if our school is indeed a welcoming place. Again, teachers need to be skilled communicators. Some parents, like some teachers, will always be more difficult to get along with than others. That's part of being human. Negative feelings can be due to personality, different learning style, or fears not expressed and dealt with. The school needs to provide a suitable process or forum for the discussion of issues causing parental concern. Severe damage can be inflicted on the inclusive process if parents feel they are not being heard.

Structuring support for parents

Just how much to involve oneself as teacher is a question often asked. As in any relationship, individuals make the difference. Some parents will need a great deal of support, some get by with just a little, like the brief chat before or after school. If the teacher feels burdened by the demands of time and energy parents are making, then it is time to step back and consider what it really is that parents are asking. Usually there are others in the school community who can help.

Certain structures such as parent–teacher meeting times, a parents' support group, regular case reviews, frequent informal discussions about individual learning programs all help to share the load. Collaborative problem-solving is an exciting way to deal with the low incidence type of learning needs with which classroom teachers are being challenged.

Giving and taking

Parents of special needs children are frequently very committed and personally involved in their child's education. They will tend to ask a lot of questions and come to visit teachers more often. They need the support and understanding of the staff, because of all the extra battles they have had to fight due to their child's needs, but mostly because it just isn't easy caring for and educating a child with an impairment, disability or deficit. Teachers need to work on developing quality relationships. Both teachers and parents need support and much can be achieved together. Mutual giving and taking of responsibility for the different things each person is good at shares the workload and empowers all through supported challenge and risk-taking; the tasks that seemed so time consuming or difficult to begin with become everyday and manageable.

The physical world
Checklist for a safe school

Physical barriers to inclusion are most often more easily solved than attitudes. There are no doubt instances you know of where ramps and railings have been installed and guide markers or lines have been painted. New buildings, of course, are now being designed with built-in wheelchair access. It doesn't take long, when one is responsible for helping a child in a wheelchair, to realise just how unfriendly and dangerous the environment can be!

Involve staff, students and parents in checking the school buildings and grounds. Then it's back to that cooperative problem-solving we keep talking about. There's no point in moaning about inadequate facilities. If the school community really wants change to happen, then it can and will happen. You just need to work together.

Some points to consider

- Are paths level and not slippery?

- Are stairs suited to the areas they service?

- Are railings fitted where necessary?

- Are there any areas where tree roots etc. have caused concrete or bitumen to become uneven?

- Are playground areas accessible to everyone?

- Do doors open the right way for wheelchair access?

- Are open doors latched back securely against the walls?

- Is furniture positioned safely? (Consider wheelchair-bound and visually impaired students.)

- Are signs and directions clearly displayed?

Who's allowed to push the wheelchair

'It's my turn!'

'No, it's not!'

'Kelly said I could push her today.'

'No, I didn't! I want to go by myself.'

Naturally, taking a turn at pushing the wheelchair has a certain status in the playground. Some children can't resist trying out anything that's new or different. Teachers should be wary of over-zealous help in pushing wheelchairs, however, as there are safety factors to be considered. A balance must be sought between safety and inclusion, between helpfulness and encouraging independence.

Depending on the wheelchair child's ability to negotiate the school environment, it may, at times or in some situations, be necessary to say, 'Only adults push the wheelchair!' For example, Kelly does not have enough strength in her arms to push herself for any distance, so depending on the day's activities, and how much time is available, and who is there to help, Kelly could be encouraged to move herself along part of the way, then ask a friend to help. If she is using her electric wheelchair, she is much more independent, and able to make more decisions for herself.

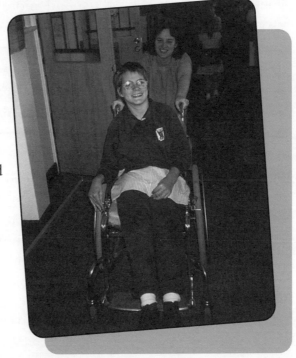

Safety conscious

Thinking ahead about possible situations will avoid unnecessary fatigue, injury or frustration. If an excursion is planned, it would be necessary for teachers to be well aware of any possible hazards or limitations the travelling or venue may present, for example alerting the railway station staff to be available for help with lifting the wheelchair plus child onto the train, checking whether all the places to be visited will be accessible. From experience we have found that many places proclaiming wheelchair accessibility are actually quite awkward to negotiate. Stress caused by having to rush is likely to cause problems like wet pants, or upset children, so forward planning to anticipate potential trouble spots, even through the average school day, will result in happier children and staff.

Helping too much vs. not enough

Ask for extra parent helpers to travel with you — just to be on the safe side. Children with special needs can tend to tire easily or become stressed in different situations, so a little extra help makes teachers and students feel so much more secure. We have also encouraged volunteer helpers at school to allow for friendly 'timeout' sessions. When impairments are always making it difficult for students to keep up with the day's activities, time spent with a volunteer tutor is time the children treasure. We brief our tutors on the types of activities we would like the children to spend more time on, and provide the resources. Careful consideration must be given to the student's needs and the personality of the tutor.

Work out the most comfortable way for children with different physical or visual challenges to negotiate stairs, doorways, corridors and classroom furniture arrangements. Able bodied people are often extremely unaware of the anxiety experienced by those who cannot move, see, hear or think quickly and coherently. Taking a drive around the school grounds in Kelly's wheelchair, for example, certainly gives an insight into how difficult the task can be, especially when cortical visual impairment has limited her sight, and the jerky hand movements caused by cerebral palsy hamper her control of the joystick. Developing safety consciousness — what do we need? —a sense of prediction. Better organisation results in less frustration.

Playtime vs. eating time — the time it takes

Ordinary things like eating can sometimes take up quite some time if concentrating on eating is a problem, or chewing and swallowing are physically difficult. Lunchtime takes more time if picking up or holding food is a problem. It's an unpleasant time if you don't really like eating at all, and you only pick at your food to stop everyone nagging. We have found it difficult to achieve the perfect balance. It's like a time and motion study that never quite works out.

One child with cerebral palsy went through a stage of not cooperating, and refused to eat very much at all for school lunch for weeks. We were very concerned, but there was not much we could do. We couldn't force-feed! Rather than make every lunchtime a misery for her, we encouraged her to eat, allowed plenty of time, then let her go to play with her friends. However, when she next visited the physiotherapist, she had made amazing gains in her physical development. In that case, and at that time, it seemed that playtime, running and jumping with her friends, was much more important than eating-time. Care, discretion and professional judgement come into play in circumstances such as these.

Supervision

Teaching assistants are most often the patient people who watch over extremely special children to be sure they don't choke or even that they actually get the food to their mouths. Teachers usually have commitments during the lunch-break such as playground supervision or meetings or phone calls to make. Teachers do need to share the experience a few times too, to be sure they understand the time it takes, and to model to other students that they have the time and patience to help. Then it happens that students will offer to sit with the special eater. It is much more inclusive to have a group of friends helping to pour out the drinks, peel the banana, unwrap the fruit bar and remind me to swallow, than to have an adult giving me total attention. Eating habits often improve when friends are encouraging a few extra mouthfuls — rather than a supervising adult. Of course, every child has different needs and supervision must be custom-built!

Playground supervisors need to be aware that very special children are in their care in the lunch-breaks. Talking about interesting or different play habits will help build up the profile or picture of the whole child.

Medication

'Is there any food left in your mouth?'

Erin pats her tummy to sign that it has all been swallowed.

'Okay. Open wide. Here it comes.'

Erin grimaces and out falls some unswallowed fruit bar along with the Tegretol tablet.

'Uh, oh! You were tricking! All that food wasn't in your tummy! Let's try again.'

A big smile from Erin and the tablet is popped in once more and slides down without any more trouble.

Positive remarks and comments usually lead to more positive results. It seems to work best for us that way. Erin's sometimes perverse sense of humour is her way of manipulating the conversation or situation. You need to have a few tricks up your sleeve when you can't talk with your voice!

Eating and medication are inextricably linked. Some special children are taking a complicated combination of different drugs and there needs to be an appropriate intake of food, at pertinent times of the day.

Monitoring should be routine and daily communication should occur between parents and the school team.

Toileting

'But this child is going to need help going to the toilet ... how are we going to cope with that?'

Our suggestion would be — quietly and calmly.

Children with special physical needs often have control problems due to poor muscle tone. Firm and consistent reminding and encouragement will gradually improve the situation.

Some children's bladder and bowel habits are very much influenced by stress. Teachers need to be aware, and limit the build-up of classroom tension. Teaching and learning cooperatively and inclusively will reduce the extra load teachers often feel is overwhelming them. Students are more responsible for the smooth and cheerful functioning of the classroom. This atmosphere is very supportive of special children.

If children need help to go to the toilet at school, there is usually aide time allowed. This would be negotiated during the enrolment process. Probably no one particularly looks forward to wiping a child's bottom or teaching a teenager how to change sanitary napkins, but these things are just a part of daily living. Try to establish clear reminder cues e.g. 'dry girl today', 'toilet time', or just a hand sign. Raising consciousness of body functioning is important in developing independence in toileting. Why would a child bother to make such conscious choices independently if there is always an adult telling you when you must go to the toilet?

In summary

With positive attitudes, acceptance and caring, differences can be seen as opportunities for growth and cooperative challenges, rather than as problems. Inclusive teaching and learning will provide for each student's quality participation, development and interaction in their own education.

All children have the right to learn, in their own way, in their own time. For **all children are special**.

Glossary

apraxia a disorder of the central nervous system characterised by impaired ability to plan and carry out a motor task

Asperger's syndrome a form of autism with sometimes extreme interest in specific areas

ataxia lack of muscular coordination – movements are jerky and uncontrolled so walking, balance and grasp are difficult

attention deficit disorder often characterised by concentration and behaviour problems

autism a developmental disability characterised by problems in social understanding, communication and interests

cerebral palsy a group of conditions characterised by motor function difficulties caused by problems with the motor control centre of the brain from brain damage at or before birth (previously known as spastic paralysis)

cortical visual impairment visual problems caused by damage to the optic nerve

Down's syndrome a genetic abnormality (previously known as mongolism) affecting mental abilities and physical features

epilepsy a disorder of the central nervous system characterised by periodic loss of consciousness with or without convulsions

psychologist studies behaviour to understand how children relate to the world

Record of interviews

School ....

Student .... Date of birth .... Home contact ....

Telephone .... Year level .... Class teacher ....

Date	Participants	Relationship to student	Issues	Action

IEP Major Goals for Term

Student .... Class ....

Date of birth .... Teacher ....

Goal	Action	Objectives		Personnel	Date Commenced	Date Reviewed
		Beginning point	Desirable end point			

IEP Action Research Plan

• Describe the issue or learning situation you want to investigate:

• What have you tried already?

• What success did you have?

• Are there other students who present with similar needs?

• What action do you want to take?

• What support will be required and from whom?

    Physical resources:

    Specialist support:

    Teaching assistant:

    Parents/adults:

    Students/peers:

• Role of action research buddy
  (possible roles: observer, reflector, team teacher, coach, resource, co-planner, etc.:

• What will be recorded and how?

• Summary of plan (include why, who, how, when, where)

Action Research Plan – Reflection Sheet

Decription of issue:

Information gathered:

Feedback:

Interpretation of feedback and data:

Implications for teacher, student, others:

Possible action:

Date .... Signed ....

Cumulative Observation Record

School ....

Student .... Date of birth ....

Home contact .... Telephone ....

Year level .... Class teacher ....

Focused Observation Records

Date	Specific skill/task	Observation/notes

Anecdotal Observation Records

Date	Specific skill/task	Observation/notes

Student Review Summary

School ....

Student .... Date of birth ....

Home contact .... Telephone ....

Year level .... Class teacher ....

Date of review .... Period of review ....

Numeracy	**Language/Communication**
Ongoing action	Ongoing action
Motor (fine-gross)	**Hearing, visual, other**
Ongoing action	Ongoing action

Student Review Summary (cont.)

Social	Behavioural
Ongoing action	**Ongoing action**

Personal – Selfcare	Parents' issues
Ongoing action	**Action arising**

Date .... Signed .... Teacher

.... Principal

.... Parent

130

Student Data Sheet

Background information: e.g. age, previous setting, etc.

Name/description of condition/difference:

How did this come about?:

Physical challenges:

Medical information:

What are this students strengthens? What can I build on?

What can you tell me about this student's parents?
Have they come to terms with their child's condition/differences/needs?
What sensitivities do I need to be aware of?

What extra support does this student need?
Is there likely to be a therapist involved?
Could these sessions happen in the classroom effectively?

Is there any specialised equipment that I need to become familiar with?

What will I need to learn?

How can you help me?

Observation Notes

Child's name .... Teacher ....

Date	Activity/lesson	Observations

Implications

Student Information Profile: Part A

School ....

Student .... Date of birth ....

Home contact .... Telephone ....

Year level .... Class teacher ....

Nature of disability	Description
Physical	
Intellectual	
Sensory	
Language	
Social	
Emotional	
Other	

Student Information Profile: Part B

Please record an appropriate level of mastery or competence.

Area		Level
Personal	Feeding	❏ Independent ❏ Minimal assistance required ❏ Moderate level of help: needs to be fed, helped with clothes, wiping ❏ Significant help needed ❏ Totally dependent: specialised help may need two people
	Toileting	❏ Independent ❏ Minimal assistance required ❏ Moderate level of help needs to be fed, helped with clothes, wiping ❏ Significant help needed ❏ Totally dependent: specialised help may need two people
Physical	Speech and Communication	❏ Normal or appropriate range ❏ Some loss: minor adjustments needed ❏ Moderate loss: may need aids or assistance ❏ Severe loss: help from aids, very limited
	Mobility	❏ Normal or appropriate range ❏ Some loss: minor adjustments needed ❏ Moderate loss: may need aids or assistance ❏ Severe loss: help from aids, very limited
	Hand functioning	❏ Normal or appropriate range ❏ Some loss: minor adjustments needed ❏ Moderate loss: may need aids or assistance ❏ Severe loss: help from aids, very limited
	Hearing	❏ Normal or appropriate range ❏ Some loss: minor adjustments needed ❏ Moderate loss: may need aids or assistance ❏ Severe loss: help from aids, very limited
	Sight	❏ Normal or appropriate range ❏ Some loss: minor adjustments needed ❏ Moderate loss: may need aids or assistance ❏ Severe loss, help from aids, very limited
Intellectual	Intellectual ability	❏ Normal or age appropriate range ❏ One year behind peers ❏ Moderate differences: 2–3 years behind peers ❏ Severe differences: 4–5 years behind peers ❏ Profound differences: more than 5 years behind peers
	Achievement	❏ Normal or age appropriate range ❏ One year behind peers ❏ Moderate differences: 2–3 years behind peers ❏ Severe differences: 4–5 years behind peers ❏ Profound differences: more than 5 years behind peers
Social/emotional	Behaviour	❏ Normal or age appropriate ❏ Some inappropriate behaviour ❏ Frequent misbehaviour, social problems ❏ Difficult: requires frequent intervention ❏ Dangerous to self and/or others
	Social relationships	❏ Normal or age appropriate ❏ Some inappropriate behaviour ❏ Frequent misbehaviour, social problems ❏ Difficult: requires frequent intervention ❏ Dangerous to self and/or others

Summary of Assessment: Part C

Language

Date	Test	Results	Comments

Mathematics

Date	Test	Results	Comments

Psychological, social, therapy, other (If applicable)

Date	Test	Results	Comments

Support services currently utilised: Part D

Nature	Contact person	Details
Speech and language therapy Occupational therapy Physiotherapy Guidance or counselling Remedial/early intervention Visiting teacher: hearing vision physical other Medical support Other		

Previous educational history: Part E

....

....

....

Date .... Signed ....

References and resources

Australian Sports Commission 1990, *Activities Manual for Children with Disabilities*, Aussie Sports Books, Pagecraft Publications, Canberra.

Armstrong, T. 1994, *Multiple Intelligence in the Classroom*, Association for Curriculum and Staff Development, Alexandria, Virginia.

Bellanca, J. & Fogarty, R. 1992, *Blueprints for Thinking in the Co-operative Classroom*, Australian edn rev. J. Dalton, Hawker Brownlow, Melbourne. (1991, IRI Skylight, Palatine, Il.)

Borba, M. & Borba, C. 1978, *Self-Esteem — A Classroom Affair: 101 Ways to Help Children Like Themselves*, Winston Press, Minneapolis.

Brigance, A. 1992, *BRIGANCE Diagnostic Comprehensive Inventory of Basic Skills*, Hawker Brownlow, Melbourne.

Canfield, J. & Wells, H. (eds) 1976, *101 Ways to Enhance Self-Concept in the Classroom: A Handbook for Teachers and Parents*, Prentice Hall, Englewood Cliffs, NJ.

Cooper, C. 1990, CLIP: Cooperative Learning Inservice Project: Developmental Studies Centre, California, presented at the AACE Conference, Tintern, Melbourne.

Dalton, J. & Boyd, J. 1991, *I Teach: A Guide to Inspiring Classroom Leadership*, Eleanor Curtain, Melbourne. (1991, Heinemann, Portsmouth, NH.)

Collis, M. & Dalton, J. 1990, *Becoming Responsible Learners: Strategies for Positive Classroom Management*, Eleanor Curtain, Melbourne. (1991, Heinemann, Portsmouth, NH.)

Gardner, H. 1983, *Frames of Mind: The Theory of Multiple Intelligence*, Basic Books, New York.

Garmston, R. 1988, 'A Call for Collegial Coaching', *The Developer*, National Staff Development Council, August, Oxford, Ohio.

Garsden, L. 1990, *Disability Awareness Kit: Activities for Primary School Students P–7*, Office of Disability, Qld Department of Family Services and Aboriginal and Islander Affairs, Brisbane.

Glasser, W. 1985, *Control Theory in the Classroom*, Harper & Row, New York.

Graves, N. & Graves, T. 1990, *A Part to Play*, Latitude Publications, Melbourne.

Harmin, M. 1994, *Inspiring Active Learning: A Handbook for Teachers*, Association for Curriculum and Staff Development, Alexandria, Virginia.

Hancock, K. & Blaby, B. 1989, *People Interacting: Self-Awareness, Communication, Social Skills and Problem Solving*, Nelson, Melbourne.

Hill, S. 1992, *Games that Work: Co-operative Games and Activities for the Primary Classroom*, Eleanor Curtain, Melbourne. (1992, Peguis Winnipeg.)

Hill, S. & Hill, T. 1990, *The Collaborative Classroom*, Eleanor Curtain, Melbourne. (1990, Heinemann, Portsmouth, NH.)

Johnson, D., Johnson, R. & Holubec, E. J. 1994, *The New Circles of Learning: Cooperation in the Classroom and School*, Association for Supervision and Curriculum Development, Alexandria, Virginia.

Kagan, S. 1990, *Cooperative Learning*, Resources for Teachers, San Capistrano, CA.

Kemp, M. 1987, *Watching Children Read and Write: Observational Records for Children with Special Needs*, Nelson, Melbourne. (1989, Heinemann, Portsmouth, NH.)

Lazear, D. 1991, *Seven Ways of Teaching: The Artistry of Teaching with Multiple Intelligences*, Skylight Publications, Palatine, Ill.

McCabe, M. E. & Rhoades, J. 1990, *The Nurturing Classroom: Developing Self-Esteem, Thinking Skills and Responsibility through Simple Cooperation*, ITA Publications, Willits, CA.

McGilp, J. & Michael, M. 1994, *The Home–School Connection: Guidelines for Working with Parents*, Eleanor Curtain, Melbourne. (1994, Heinemann, Portsmouth, NH.)

McGrath, H. & Francey, S. 1991, *Friendly Kids, Friendly Classrooms: Teaching Social Skills and Confidence in the Classroom*, Longman, Melbourne.

McGrath, H. & Noble, T. 1993, *Different Kids, Same Classroom*, Longman, Melbourne.

Mann, K. 1991, *Breaking Down the Barriers*, CDC Tasmanian Education Department, Published by Curriculum Development Centre, Canberra

Manning, M. L. & Lucking, R. 1991, 'The what, why and how of cooperative learning', *The Clearing House*, vol. 64, no. 3, Jan/Feb.

Moorman, C. 1993, *Managing Student Outcomes through Co-operative Learning*, Performance Learning Systems, Nevada City CA.

Moorman, C. & Dishon, D. 1982, *Our Classroom: We Can Learn Together*, Personal Power Press, Bay City, Mich.

Principles of Effective Learning and Teaching, 1994, Department of Education, Studies Directorate Publishing Services, Brisbane.

Putnam, J. 1991, 'Curriculum adaptations for students with disabilities in co-operative groups', *Cooperative Learning*, IASCE, Santa Cruz, CA, vol. 12, no. 1, pp. 8–11.

Reasoner, R. 1986, *Building Self-Esteem*, Consulting Psychologists Press, Palo Alto CA.

Sanders, P. 1991, *Let's Talk about Disabled People*, Gloucester Press, London. (1992, Grolier, Danberry, CT)

Sapon-Shevin, M. 1990, 'Schools as communities of love and caring', *Holistic Education Review*, Summer.

Sapon-Shevin, M. 1991, 'Cooperative learning in inclusive classrooms: learning to become a community', *Cooperative Learning*, IASCE, Santa Cruz, CA, vol. 12, no. 1, p. 10.

Topping, K. 1988, *Peer Tutoring Handbook: Promoting Co-operative Learning*, Brookline Books, Cambridge MA.

Villa, R. et al. 1992, *Restructuring for Caring and Effective Education: An Administrative Strategic Guide to Creating Heterogenous Schools*, Brooks Publishing, Baltimore.

Walker, D. & Brown, P. 1994, *Pathways to Co-operation: Starting Points for Co-operative Learning*, Eleanor Curtain, Melbourne, (1994, Peguis, Winnipeg.)

Wilson, J. & Egeberg, P. 1990, *Co-operative Challenges and Student Investigations*, Nelson, Melbourne.

Wing Jan, L. & Wilson, J. 1993, *Thinking for Themselves: Developing Strategies for Reflective Learning*, Eleanor Curtain, Melbourne. (1993, Heinemann, Portsmouth, NH.)

Index

action research 73–4
    plan and reflection sheets
        75–6, 79, 125
anecdotal records 92
awareness meetings 86–90
awareness raising 85–90
    with children 98–9
    with parents and community
        99–101

basic needs of children 28–35
    belonging 29–32
    enjoyment 33
    freedom 32–3
    safety 35
    valuing 34–5
behaviour management 46–50
    covenants, rules, norms 47–9
    giving directions 49–50
    recognition 50
belonging 29–32
    personal classroom 30
    physical environment 29–30
    welcoming classroom 31, 46
broadening teaching practice
    4–7, 20

collaborative learning 52–64
cooperative learning 53–9
    benefits of 53–4
    essential elements of 54–8
    and inclusion 58–9
covenants 47–8
cumulative observation record
    80, 82–3, 127–8
curriculum adaptation 64–9
    lower level expectations 68–9
    modified presentation 66–7
    modified student response 65
    reduced workload 67

difference 3–7

effective teaching and learning,
    principles of 25–6, 36–41
enjoyment 33

freedom 32–3
friendship 14–15

IEP major goals 75, 78, 124
inclusion 1, 16–22
    background to 16–18
    benefits of 20
    core element of 24–5
    inclusive practice 110–11
    preparing for 85–101
    principles of 19
inclusive playgrounds 7–11
inclusive classrooms 1, 18–22,
    23–36
    core elements 42–3
    elements for building 1
    essential elements 21
    influences on 24
    managing the environment
        38–9
    preparing for 26, 70
individual education programs
    69–84
    action research, plan and
        reflection sheets 75–6, 79,
        125
    cumulative observation record
        80, 82–3, 127–8
    forms and processes 72–3,
        74–84
    IEP major goals 75, 78, 124
    record of interviews 75, 77,
        123
    student review summary 80,
        84, 129–30
    support and resources 71–2
    teacher's role 71
integration 17

learning partnerships 39–40

mainstreaming 1, 17
management and organisation
    41–51
meaningful learning 37
medication 120

mentoring 62–4
modelling play 7–10
norms 48–9
nurturing 21

obsessions 13–14

parent helpers 118
peer tutoring 60–1
peer helpers 110
peer tutoring 20–1
physical environments 29–30,
    44–6, 116–21
    safety checklist 116–17
playing 7–8
preparation for inclusion 26, 37,
    85–101
proximal development 21

reciprocity 20, 58
record of interviews 75, 77, 123
recording
    importance of 91–8
    sharing records 101
rituals 13–14
role play 13
rules 47

safety 35, 116–17
social and cultural contexts 41
social skills 11–13
special needs 1, 16
    checklist for teachers 27
    definition 1
student information profiles 94–8
student review summary 80, 84,
    129–30
supervision 119
support
    for parents 112–16
    for teachers 71–2, 105–109
toileting 120–1
touch 51

valuing 34–5

wheelchairs 102–3, 117

Inclusive Classrooms From A to Z
A handbook for educators
Gretchen Goodman

In this thoroughly practical book Gretchen Goodman helps primary grade teachers move step-by-step toward creating more inclusive classrooms. Having made that change in her own teaching, she understands the kind of support teachers need as they make a similar transition.

She aims to provide direct guidance to teachers who are striving to achieve their vision of inclusive schools as places where all children can experience success, develop lifelong friendships, and gain skills that enable them to become contributing members of society.

The book offers background information on inclusion, hands-on activities and strategies for immediate implementations, and blackline forms, masters, and checklists to get the process started. Literally an 'a-to-z' compendium, it covers such topics as acceptance, lesson adaptation, creating individualised education programs, support personnel, and common developmental expectations. Throughout she stresses that inclusion is a process of gradual change toward quality education and quality life for all.

Teacher's Publishing Group

216pp Paperback   1-57110-200-0

The Parent Project
A workshop approach to parent involvement
James Vopat, Carroll College and *The Milwaukee Writing Project*

Involving parents in their children's schooling is a matter of intense concern in North America. Teachers and administrators want to construct a program that creates positive involvement. This is especially critical for Chapter I schools that are mandated to use a portion of their funds for home-and-school programs.

Jim Vopat's *The Parent Project* offers a framework built on the fact that school has changed dramatically since most parents were there. He believes that parental involvement should strengthen the link between home and school, and to achieve this goal parents need to be introduced to the revitalised school classroom. *The Parent Project* calls on the most powerful aspects of school reform — workshops, journals, cooperative groups, shared reading, agenda building, interviewing, goal setting, and critical thinking. These are classroom learning strategies experienced by children every day yet are unfamiliar to their parents. But when parents have the opportunity to work with these strategies, they are able to understand them and discover how to support them.

Using a workshop/process model, parents become involved with their children's classroom activities and are thus empowered to support their children's education. These workshops ensure participant ownership of a program's overall agenda while providing long-term structures for support and continued development. They may be implemented as described here, or, preferably, adapted to suit the needs of individual communities.

The Parent Project is the result of a five-year collaboration between Chapter I directors, progressive elementary teachers, social workers, and parent coordinators and aides in the Milwaukee city schools. Filled with persuasive and authentic publications between parents and their children, this book will appeal to all teachers and administrators who want to work as equal partners with parents to involve them in, and inform them about, their children's education.

Stenhouse Publishers

208pp Paperback   1-57110-001-6

Learning to See
Assessment through observation

Mary Jane Drummond, Cambridge Institute of Education
Foreword by Gordon Wells, Ontario Institute for Students in Education

'... in this profound and inspiring book, Mary Jane Drummond succeeds in persuading us that to focus on assessment is indeed to get to the heart of education.'
from the Foreword by Gordon Wells

'What emerges from Drummond's book is a clear and practical theory, from which teachers can truly create new approaches to assessment.'
from a pre-publication review by Ruth Hubbard

Unlike much work on assessment that has appeared lately, this book goes beyond alternative techniques and instruments and proposes that accurate assessment must begin with close observation of children and that teachers must understand the children's learning before they can begin any accurate assessment. Drummond believes that children have a right to education, and teachers can only meet their responsibilities for children through judicious assessment based on observation in all subjects. She argues that assessment is not simply an objective or mechanical task, but a process involving the subjective perceptions of the teacher in which an understanding of children's learning can be used to create and improve curriculum.

Learning to See is illuminated with first-hand accounts of children's learning, taken from the author's research, from practising teachers' studies of their classrooms and students, and from the work of such significant figures as Paul Light, L.S. Vygotsky, and Margaret Donaldson. Thus, teachers will find a basis in theory to support this thoughtful approach to assessment, which examines holistically what children bring to their schooling and explores ways of helping them derive the most from it.

An excellent choice for inservice or preservice training, *Learning to See* will be welcomed by anyone with a professional interest in ensuring that assessment is made to work in the interests of children.

Stenhouse Publishers

208pp Paperback   1-57110-004-0